Counseling Troubled Youth

Counseling and Pastoral Theology

Andrew D. Lester, Series Editor

Counseling Troubled Youth

Robert C. Dykstra

Westminster John Knox Press
Louisville, Kentucky

Grateful acknowledgment is made to the following for permission to
reprint copyrighted material:
HarperCollins Publishers, from Leroy Aarons, *Prayers for Bobby:
A Mother's Coming to Terms with the Suicide of Her Gay Son,*
copyright © 1995 by Leroy Aarons.

The Urban Institute Press, from "The Story of John Turner,"
by Elijah Anderson, in *Drugs, Crime, and Social Isolation: Barriers to
Urban Opportunity*, edited by Adele V. Harrell and George E.
Peterson, copyright © 1992 The Urban Institute.

Book design by Jennifer K. Cox
Cover design by Kevin Darst

First Edition
Published by Westminster John Knox Press
Louisville, Kentucky

This book is printed on acid-free paper that meets the
American National Standards Institute Z39.48 standard. ∞

PRINTED IN THE UNITED STATES OF AMERICA
99 00 01 02 03 04 05 06 — 10 9 8 7 6 5 4 3 2

Library of Congress Cataloging-in-Publication Data
Dykstra, Robert C., date.
    Counseling troubled youth / by Robert C. Dykstra. — 1st ed.
        p.   cm. — (Counseling and pastoral theology)
    Includes bibliographical references and index.
    ISBN 0-664-25654-6 (alk. paper)
    1. Problem youth—Pastoral counseling of.   I. Title.   II. Series.
BV4464.5.D95   1997
259'.23—dc21   97-20101

for the Rev. Henry E. Fawcett,
with gratitude to God

Contents

Foreword

Pastors and pastoral counselors who offer care to young people feel their pain and are often overwhelmed by what Robert Dykstra calls their "confusing and treacherous" journey. Isaiah's words, "Even youths will faint and be weary, and the young will fall exhausted," are an apt description of today's adolescents. Both the collective statistics and the individual stories of suicide, homicide, eating disorders, drugs, alcohol, promiscuity, school failures, and other destructive symptoms are frightening. Furthermore, this youthful discontent is manifested regardless of ethnic heritage, sex, or socioeconomic status.

Making sense of this terrible destruction, says Dykstra, leads us to look at the underlying causes. What is the central issue? Dykstra takes us to the heart of the matter when he says "the suffering . . . reflects a widespread loss of hope or faith in a meaningful future." Going beneath the specific manifestations of this despair among youth, he explores questions about what is happening to the "self." What are the "intrapsychic, cultural, and spiritual forces" that demand our theological reflection? He uses the concepts of developmental object relations theory (from James F. Masterson) and self psychology (from Heinz Kohut) as conversational partners with the Christian doctrine of hope (from Jürgen Moltmann).

Out of this dialogue Dykstra develops a unique pastoral theological perspective on adolescent process that he calls "the eschatological self"— "a theological way of expressing the self's experience of newness, surprise, and hope." The term eschatological self captures his conviction that the future coming at us is as important as our past and present, our "coming" as important as our "becoming." This work shows us how to understand trouble in young people as rooted in the inability to keep past and future in tension, resulting in "apathetic despair" or "alienation from any future."

Dykstra's purpose is to help pastoral caregivers in "birthing or restoring wholeness and integrity" to youth by giving us the theoretical knowledge and practical wisdom to offer effective ministry during their journey. Not only does the reader receive easily understandable descriptions of this material, but four extensive case studies are included as illustration.

The *Counseling and Pastoral Theology* Series

The purpose of this series is to address clinical issues that arise among particular populations currently neglected in the literature on pastoral care and counseling (women in lesbian relationships, African American couples, adolescents under stress, women who are depressed, survivors of sexual abuse, adult adoptees, persons with terminal illness, and couples experiencing infertility). This series is committed to enhance both the theoretical base and the clinical expertise of pastoral caregivers by providing a pastoral theological paradigm that will inform both assessment and intervention with persons in these specific populations.

Many books in pastoral care and counseling are more carefully informed by the behavioral and social sciences than by classical theological disciplines. Pastoral care and counseling specialists have been criticized for ignoring our theological heritage and challenged to reevaluate our idolization of psychology and to claim our unique perspectives on the human predicament. The discipline of pastoral theology has made significant strides in the last decade. The Society for Pastoral Theology was formed in 1985 and now publishes the *Journal of Pastoral Theology*.

Pastoral theology grows out of data gathered from at least three sources: (1) revelation about the human condition uncovered by the social and behavioral sciences, (2) wisdom from the classical theological disciplines, and (3) insight garnered from reflection on the pastoral ministry event. The development of pastoral theology grows out of the dialogue between these three perspectives, each perspective enabled to ask questions of, challenge, and critique the other perspectives.

Each author is clinically experienced and academically prepared to write about the particular population with which she or he is personally concerned and professionally involved. Each author develops a "constructive pastoral theology," developing the theological frame of reference that provides the unique perspective from which a pastoral person approaches both assessment and intervention. This constructive pastoral theology will enable clinically trained pastors and pastoral care specialists (pastoral counselors, chaplains, Clinical Pastoral Education supervisors) to creatively participate in pastoral relationships that effectively enable healing, sustaining, guiding, reconciling, and liberating.

Though the focus will be on offering pastoral care and counseling to individuals, couples, and families, each author is cognizant of the interaction between individuals and their environment. These books will consider the effects of larger systems, from family of origin to cultural constructs. Each author will use case material from her or his clinical pastoral ministry to focus the reader's attention on the issues faced by the particular population as viewed from the pastoral theological paradigm.

My thanks to colleagues who faithfully served on the Advisory Committee and expended many hours of creative work to ensure that this series would make a substantial contribution: Bonnie Miller-McLemore (1992–1996), Nancy Ramsay (1992–1996), Han van den Blink (1992–1994), Larry Graham (1994–1996), and Linda Kirkland-Harris (1994–1996).

Andrew D. Lester
Brite Divinity School

Acknowledgments

This book, like the eschatological self it seeks to describe, issues from the gracious workings of God and many persons in my life, only some of whom can be acknowledged here. Donald Capps, my teacher in pastoral theology at Princeton Theological Seminary, read through many manuscript drafts and offered discerning suggestions with patience and care. Timothy Staveteig, an editor formerly with Westminster John Knox Press, shepherded this venture at the outset, and Jon Berquist saw it through to its conclusion. Series editor Andrew Lester supplied continuing guidance as well.

Leanne Van Dyk, Rodney Hunter, Ane Fitzgerald, and Bradley Longfield read various earlier versions and enhanced the book with insights from their respective fields of systematic and pastoral theology, feminist counseling theory, and church history. I am grateful also to students and colleagues at the University of Dubuque Theological Seminary, especially Dean Jeffrey Bullock, who makes space for his faculty to write, and Elizabeth Platt, whose enthusiasm for the eschatological self sustained me in the writing.

Although with the exception of Bobby Griffith they remain anonymous here, I am indebted to those youth who have entrusted their stories and struggles in the case studies of the book. My wife, Molly, also deserves heartfelt thanks, not only for keen editorial skills and theological queries concerning this project but also for freely sharing of herself with me down other paths that we travel together. My mother, Betty Hugunin, along with James and Mary McNelis and the other members of our family, have offered ongoing support as well. I wish finally to thank my pastor, the Rev. Henry E. Fawcett, and his wife, VeNita, who in my youth opened new vistas of Christian faith and sought to raise me with wings like eagles.

Robert C. Dykstra

Dubuque, Iowa
Epiphany 1997

Even youths will faint and
be weary,
and the young will fall
exhausted;
but those who wait for the LORD
shall renew their strength,
they shall mount up with wings
like eagles,
they shall run and not be weary,
they shall walk and not faint.
—Isaiah 40:30–31 (NRSV)

Introduction

Isaiah writes that "even youths will faint and be weary, and the young will fall exhausted," poetic words that speak to the vulnerability of youth in all times and places, but that seem especially poignant in capturing the predicament of American young people at the close of the twentieth century. Widespread statistical and anecdotal evidence for such weariness and exhaustion, such "fainting," among contemporary youth confirms what so many intuitively suspect: that in recent decades something has gone awry, has changed or is changing still for those attempting to navigate their way from childhood to adulthood. The journey looms far more confusing and treacherous today for significant numbers of American youth, who embody a kind of suffering that, while varying greatly in its outward manifestations, collectively reflects a widespread loss of hope or faith in a meaningful future as well as a dislocation from any historical past—what many now are calling disorders of the "self."

Even a cursory glance at recent numbers gives cause for deep concern. Figures from the National Center for Health Statistics, for example, show that in 1990, 12,223 youth between the ages of fifteen and twenty-four in the United States died from suicide or homicide, thirty-four deaths each day. Young men account for 85 percent of these deaths, fully two-thirds to three-quarters of them involving firearms. The United States ranks first among twenty developed nations in aggregate suicide and homicide rates for this age group.[1] From 1985 to 1991, the annual rate at which adolescent males ages fifteen to nineteen died by homicide increased 154 percent, while rates for other age groups remained level.[2] The toll is especially grim among minority youth, ten times as likely to die a violent death as young whites. According to a recent report from the Centers for Disease Control in Atlanta, "in some areas of the country it is now more likely for a black male between his fifteenth and twenty-fourth birthdays to die from homicide than it was for a U.S. soldier to be killed on a tour of duty in Vietnam."[3]

In 1995, one in three African American men in their twenties was under the supervision of the criminal justice system.[4]

Homicides and suicides account for only a portion of adolescent deaths in this country each year. Accidents claimed an additional 17,000 youthful lives in 1988, most of these involving motor vehicles. In one-half of these, the driver had a blood alcohol level twice the normal legal limit. In one recent study, one-third of eighth-grade students and 44 percent of tenth-grade students reported having ridden in a car during the previous month with a driver under the influence of alcohol or drugs.[5] Another study suggests that many accidents among adolescents—including one-car accidents and even seemingly unintentional injuries and assaults—may often be subtly disguised suicide attempts or warnings. The researchers found the incidence of suicide twelve times higher among youth previously hospitalized because of an injury.[6]

Other signs of devastation and despair among youth continue to mount. According to the 1990 Census Bureau survey, one in four children under age eighteen lives in a one-parent household, this proportion having doubled in the past two decades, in turn increasing the likelihood of poverty. In 1969, 13.5 percent of six- to seventeen-year-olds lived in poverty, increasing by 1986 to 20 percent of this age group and, by 1989, to nearly 25 percent of children under six years of age.[7] Pregnancy rates among American teenagers are among the highest of the developed nations, with 1.1 million young women ages fifteen to nineteen, roughly one in ten adolescent girls, becoming pregnant in 1991, this more than double and triple the 1965 and 1950 rates, respectively.[8]

Additional troubling data concerning sexual abuse, sexually transmitted diseases, eating disorders, and youthful crime could be added to this brief survey. While one-half of the children in this country will navigate the waters of youth with relative facility, as many as one in four is at great risk.[9] Beyond more normative stressors such as the biological changes of puberty or adjusting to new school environments, these youth typically experience heightened stress from some combination of persistent parental marital discord or divorce, loss of or separation from a parent, parental psychiatric disorders, childhood abuse, being placed in the care of local authorities, minority status, paternal criminality, chronic illness, or a low level of parental education.[10] A host of these and other indicators suggests something subtly or grossly amiss for millions of contemporary youth, for whom the adult culture is increasingly inhospitable and the passage to public life somehow more foreboding.

As children attempting to gain entrance into the adult world of cultural and sexual relations, adolescents stand at one of the most dramatic of human crossroads and are the group developmentally most vulnerable to the ambiguities of the culture to which they aspire. The particular forms of difficulties among youth in any specific time and place thus serve in part as a sensitive barometer of the unique cultural ambivalences of that society. When young people literally begin to destroy themselves and others in unprecedented numbers—suggesting that for many death is the more "viable" alternative to the future offered them by their culture—we must question not only what is happening in these youth individually, but also what leads their culture to exact for its own survival the sacrifice of its children and youth. Any attempt to understand and respond to the peculiar disorders of contemporary American young people requires some account as well of the "disorders" of these various environments that coalesce in the selves or souls of the youth.

No one perspective on a subject so vast as adolescence in current culture or so intricate as the unique self of any individual young person can claim to offer more than a limited and partial understanding. To attempt to give a particular sort of voice to adolescent suffering, as this book seeks to do, inevitably means that other equally or even more compelling voices risk going unheard. Yet recognizing the inevitability of such subjectivity, in my view, in no way reduces the objective urgency of adolescent suffering. Millions of American young people are confronting severe troubles and stand in need of help, regardless of varying and relative theoretical perspectives on their problems. Their anguish or apathy stand in judgment of cultural complacency and Christian witness alike, demanding some kind of entrance into these dilemmas, however limited, in a spirit of humility and repentance.

In the theological enterprise, such entrance into the lives of children and youth characteristically has come under the domain of Christian educators, with adolescents generally overlooked in pastoral counseling literature. Those pertinent pastoral counseling texts available typically attempt a topical strategy, identifying potential problem areas such as drugs and drinking, sexual activity, failure in school, communication with parents, or suicide, and suggesting ways pastors or churches might address each topic with their young people.[11] The value and sensibilities of these practical texts should not be disparaged. Yet they leave the theologically trained reader yearning for a more unified understanding of youth and their problems and for coherent theological reflection linking these destructive problems with intrapsychic, cultural, and spiritual forces. It is this kind of understanding we seek here, centering around a pastoral theological exploration of the adolescent self.

This book does not evade troubling dilemmas of addiction, sexual abuse and confusion, suicide, and other topics so often rightly at the center of concern in adolescent counseling literature. It attempts to show that these and other problems reflect even more fundamental traumas of the contemporary self and culture that can orient our pastoral response. In terms of their experience of self, a wealthy suburban anorexic girl and an inner-city boy encompassed by drug wars may have far more in common than their divergent social situations and symptoms suggest. If pastoral counselors can begin to articulate a psychologically sensitive theology of the self, they may be freed from the impossible expectation of having to become experts on every conceivable problem experienced by particular young people in their care. They then may enter such lives more confident of their ability to provide understanding and intervention for change, even while recognizing that in so entering they themselves risk being changed by the encounter.

Physicians of the Soul

Amid the vast sea of specialties and subspecialties in various helping disciplines, the unique task of pastors and pastoral care specialists may well be that of birthing or restoring wholeness and integrity in persons atomized by an often depersonalizing, professionalized culture. Theirs is the very general specialty of what pastoral theologian Rodney Hunter described as helping persons learn how to live with life's transcending limits of evil, death, and meaninglessness as destructive of the self but not ultimate for the self. The pastoral task thus involves helping a person learn

> something like how to receive one's existence from God beyond life and death, beyond righteousness and sin, beyond meaning and meaninglessness, and thus how to live transcendently as a child of God.[12]

What kind of expertise is this? I suggest that it may be in part an expertise of the psyche, of the self or soul. If pastoral work involves, as characterized historically, the *cura animarum*, the care of souls, then pastors need somehow to be experts of the self, of its nature and functioning, its sicknesses and salvations. This preoccupation with the self initially may strike modern pastoral sensibilities as excessively individualistic or privatistic, as neglectful of arenas of community and context. I seek rather to propose an understanding of the self that, attentive to such protests, recognizes and restores its broader constituents.

The troubling statistics already cited represent, of course, specific youth in actual families, neighborhoods, and communities. So we wonder, Are there certain experiences of self that, without negating important contextual differences, nevertheless may unite young people across lines of gender, race, social class, or religious belief? Can the self ever be so known or shared?

I came to ask such questions out of my own pastoral work with youth in quite diverse spheres—in wealthy suburban congregations in the Midwest and Northwest, in small Native American fishing villages in Alaska, in a working-class congregation and a maximum-security state prison in the urban East, in an adolescent psychiatric hospital in downtown Chicago. In each of these distinctive settings, I found myself facing youth with backgrounds and experiences far different than I myself encountered as an adolescent growing up in a nurturing Presbyterian home and congregation in an all-white, rural Minnesota town. In addition to dozens of happy memories from my work with these youth, I also recall the painful moments of suicide attempts (and one completion) among the suburban youth, gunshot wounds among the urban youth, and a wide array of lesser crises in between.

My work with young people from these very different contexts forced me to consider my own youth through startlingly new sets of lenses. Yet as these experiences began to accumulate, I found myself undergoing something of a figure/ground shift: the contextual newness and differences began to recede, while a faint sense of their similarities to one another and to myself began to emerge. I found myself again and again coming to wonder, what was subtly comparable about these very diverse young people. Even more disconcerting, why were their struggles and dilemmas so much like my own, not just in my adolescence, but even then as a young adult, even now still? Why were the wealthy suburban white youth often as apathetic and hopeless, as condemned to the immediacy of their present experiences and as self-involved and yet self-loathing, as were the urban African American youth serving endless years in prison or facing life paralyzed by a bullet, or as were those Native American youth who sensed that no world would welcome them beyond the borders of their tiny villages? What might account for seemingly parallel and in too many cases desolate affective experiences of young people from such different stations in life? Such were the questions that led to the present investigation of the adolescent self.

For the past several years I have taught a seminary course on pastoral care and counseling with adolescents. One assignment for that course has required that each student become a sort of anthropologist of adolescence by conducting three one-hour interviews with any one young person outside the student's own family. I provide a list of potential interview questions—playful questions but also significant ones concerning sexuality, death, and experiences of God—to which the students add their own creative possibilities. They are instructed not to attempt to counsel the adolescent in the interviews but more simply to learn of the young person's history, struggles, views, hopes, and faith. The interviews are tape-recorded and subsequently fully transcribed into a lengthy verbatim manuscript. In a final semester paper, the student reflects on and analyzes those conversations using various theoretical materials and personal insights from the course.

In this exercise, I often find myself struck by two observations. The first occurs on the opening day of the semester, when it becomes evident that this assignment makes many students anxious. The threat inherent in the thought of actually talking at length with a young person becomes quite palpable. The second observation, which comes only at the end of the semester, is more striking. As I near the end of reading each transcription and reach the point where the seminarian thanks the young person for granting the interview, almost invariably the youth will respond by saying something like, "That's OK. I sort of enjoyed it. No adult has ever just listened to me for three hours before."

Although I have read a response similar to this in many such interviews, I always find myself deeply moved by it. While I am grateful that my student and I have been allowed to plumb the depths of this youthful life, I also am saddened to learn that no other adult, at least outside and perhaps inside the young person's family, has ever done so. This is a common conclusion to these interviews with youth across a diverse spectrum of gender, race, class, faith, and family backgrounds. No adult previously has listened to them for three hours.

We need not romanticize or idealize youth, nor relinquish our roles as spiritual mentors or cultural guarantors, nor even indulge their demands and tantrums, to acknowledge something amiss in this response. Even as they are always among the first to die on the front lines of one nation's political wars against another, so too are youth typically first eclipsed in the emotional and spiritual cross fire between or within sparring factions of their various familial, cultural, and ecclesial communities.

What would physicians of the soul hear if we were to listen at length to the stories of youth who, against considerable odds, have managed to survive, or of those even who have fainted and succumbed? Would we not expect to find in them a clearer, more pristine mirror of our own selves, and of the culture and congregations in which we labor? Might we not detect indictments of this culture's unspoken willingness to sacrifice thousands of its young to the voracious appetites of its false, often invisible gods? Or discover in them as well evidence of God's Spirit seeking to rescue, sustain, and open them to more hopeful horizons of faith and future?

This book contends that pastoral care specialists occupy a unique, even enviable, position for addressing these and other pressing questions concerning youth in crisis. As heirs to and stewards of the sometimes healing, sometimes destructive doctrines and rituals of the Christian heritage, pastoral workers labor to discern the Spirit's stirrings, to honor and refashion the mysteries and wisdom of faith for a new generation. The present study centers its efforts at such theological discernment around the relevance for despairing youth and beleaguered pastors of promising recent research concerning eschatology, the doctrine of Christian hope. Eschatological hope, born of faith in the cross and resurrection of Jesus Christ, inspires in its constituents a kind of hope against hope, a hope that, despite all appearances to the contrary and against all odds in our work with difficult youth, clings to the promises of God and the possibility of transformation and new life.

Physicians of the soul additionally recognize that even the most divine of revelations or esoteric doctrinal formulations entrusted us by our faith traditions includes at least some psychological component, having emerged from what was once for some person or community a quickening of the human heart, a gladdening or terrifying encounter with the presence or absence of God, a wrenching experience of alienation from friend or foe, a visitation of death or new life. In this regard, recent psychology, particularly depth psychology, often enlivens our efforts at theological reflection and pastoral intervention as it seeks to assist suffering persons who face conscious and unconscious predicaments. Explorations of the self's development, distortions, and healing have been at the heart of much theoretical and clinical work in depth psychology for the past several decades. While a diverse range of other psychological theories—from person-centered to family systems to problem-solving as well as paradoxical approaches—also vitally contributes to our work with youth in crisis, our concern for the nuances of the adolescent self leads to a more explicit focus here on the lively debates of recent developmental object relations theory and self psychology.

The task of theology, poignantly described recently as "an aspect of the continuing repentance" of the church,[13] necessarily involves giving audience not only to those who speak in the specialized vernacular of, say, systematic theology or depth psychology, but additionally to those who frequently suffer in silence, here the confused, often critical tongues of troubled youth themselves. The life stories of four particular young people facing quite desperate straits comprise the pivotal core of this study.

Some may contend that the severity of these cases creates a caricatured portrait of contemporary young people, an objection perhaps justified by the fact that the youth described here came to the attention of therapists or the judicial system. Although sympathetic to this concern, I have found the difference between these and seemingly ordinary youths to be one more of degree than of kind. As these young people's stories of suffering unfold in some detail, the patient reader may well discover in them, as I have, a resonant and disconcerting familiarity. They seem to beg our pastoral humility and "continuing repentance," by demonstrating the uncanny ability of any particular youth to expose the limitations of every theory or perspective, including the one proposed in this book. More constructively, the presence and candor of these youthful voices provide acid-test cases by which to assess any hopeful strategies of intervention and change.

What emerges from this convergence of recent theology, psychology, and actual stories of young people is a way of envisioning the self that I have come to call the "eschatological self," which, I trust, will afford pastors renewed patience, courage, and hope against hope in caring for youth who fall exhausted.

The Plan of the Book

A final introductory word is in order concerning the book's design. Chapter 1 considers the familiar yet elusive construct of the self and its contemporary afflictions. It also provides entrance into conversations concerning eschatology in recent theology and offers a preliminary sketch of the eschatological self.

Chapters 2 through 5 comprise Part I of the book, in which developmental psychologies are brought to bear upon the young person's "becoming" a self through the intricate process of negotiating, or failing to negotiate, entrance into the myriad complexities of adult life and culture. Chapter 2 offers the first of two forays into depth psychology, critically examining the developmental object relations theory of James F. Masterson in assisting so-called borderline adolescents. Chapter 3 in turn employs Masterson's theory as the initial analytical lens for an extended case study of Stan (a pseudonym), a suburban youth whose veneer of boyish charm and indifference proves increasingly ineffective in quelling his overwhelming anxiety and despair. Chapter 4 summarizes the influential self psychology of Heinz Kohut in treating narcissistic disorders, followed in chapter 5 by a second case study initially considered in terms of Kohut's work. There, John Turner (another pseudonym), a handsome youth imperturbable among his peers on the streets of urban Philadelphia, finds himself distressingly vulnerable when confronting the criminal justice system. In a pivotal moment of desperation, he beseeches the aid of a kindly but unsuspecting stranger, a sociologist named Elijah Anderson.

Part II of the book, consisting of the final three chapters and epilogue, conceives of the youthful self as not only maturing gradually through time, as in Part I, but also as "coming," as being delivered, often through singular moments of surprising and rapid transformation, from the young person's "future" as well. Chapter 6 elaborates on the eschatological self outlined previously in chapter 1, but in relation to the psychological theorists and case studies of Part I. This new understanding of the self is then tested against two additional case studies of despondent youth. In chapter 7, we meet Laurie (also a pseudonym), a sixteen-year-old Midwestern girl sexually abused throughout her childhood and now increasingly adept at abusing herself and others, yet unresponsive to multiple therapeutic efforts on her behalf. In chapter 8, we consider the wrenching story of Bobby Griffith (his actual name), a gay youth raised in a conservative and covertly conflicted Christian home, who at the age of twenty, having failed to reconcile his faith and sexual desires, finally took his own life. The epilogue offers concluding convictions concerning our labors on behalf of weary youth, and theirs on ours, to the end that youth and counselors alike may, in Isaiah's poetry, "mount up with wings like eagles, . . . run and not be weary, . . . walk and not faint."

Chapter One

The Self
amid Symptoms
of Youthful Despair

I'm not afraid of death. You could put a gun to my head, and I wouldn't be afraid. I'm not afraid of death. I'm already dead.

—*Eighteen-year-old, to the author*

The self is a familiar mystery. It is an elusive thing, a bead of mercury always just beyond grasp, a horizon never quite reached. We talk frequently and casually about ourselves in everyday conversation without consciously considering the "self" to which we refer: "I just wasn't myself at that party last night," or "I can't seem to make myself do what I know that I have to do," or "I have never felt so much myself as during my college years," or even, tucked in the epigraph quote, "I'm already dead." Self-referential language is an ordinary part of our communication, the self a commonplace notion.

At those times when we become more self-conscious, whether through unexpected exposure or intentional self-reflection, the mysterious qualities of this close companion begin to surface. Just who or what is this *self* that was at odds with one's *I* at the party last night, or that refuses to do what *I* think that it ought, or that so thoroughly relished its college years, or that with devastating lucidity can articulate its own untimely death? To reflect upon such questions quickly envelopes the self in peculiar convolutions. Like the expert pianist or typist whose fingers begin to stumble only upon becoming consciously aware of them, the self quickly runs up against the limits of its expansiveness when contemplating its own selfhood. What in mundane discourse is one's intimate companion becomes suddenly an enigmatic stranger. The self, at once both the subject as well as the object of its study, cannot finally fully capture or contain itself. It is a familiar mystery.

At once ordinary and unusual, both local and expansive, the self cuts across artificially drawn barriers between the disciplines, a subject of investigation for theology and psychology alike, as well as a subject of vital interest to youth unconcerned about theoretical speculations yet experts nonetheless in self-examination. Any particular young person is as much an authority on the subject of the adolescent self as the highly learned theologian or psychologist, making for a rather remarkable leveling of the playing field, a refreshing check to any exclusive claims to truth.

Because these mysterious and mercurial capacities of the self resist the captivity of any one understanding, the theoretical speculations on the self explored throughout this book comprise only a glimpse of its total experience. But they do reflect a convergence of perspectives from recent theology, psychology, and adolescent life that promises a unique vantage into the nature and care of young people.

Many theorists from a wide range of disciplines have sought to understand the troubled self of wealthy Western nations, using a variety of terms to try to describe it. It has been called the narcissistic self, the borderline self, the fragmented self, the tragic self, the apathetic self, the protean self, the survivor self, the egocentric self, the minimal self, the depleted self, the split self, and the postmodern self. Scholars have approached the problem of the contemporary self from diverse theoretical presuppositions, attributing the origins of its suffering to wide-ranging sources and prescribing a broad array of solutions. But what is striking is the unanimity they have achieved when actually describing the phenomenological attributes of the suffering persons. If anything unites the young people whose lives constitute current troubling statistics of adolescent despair and death, it is likely these very attributes that the theorists have struggled to name. Among the most frequently mentioned and significant are

1. A dislocation from one's ancestral roots and traditions, or from any historical past, as well as a loss of hope or faith in a meaningful future, resulting in a focus on present, here-and-now experience and immediate gratification.

2. A sense of malaise, apathy, passivity, depression or "psychic numbing"; a sense of helplessness or powerlessness in controlling anything but one's own subjective experiences or destiny, themselves seemingly beyond control.

3. A vague and diffuse sense of rage, shame, and guilt, compounded by an inability to identify specific targets for these feelings in order thereby to control them.

4. A movement away from the turn-of-the-century preoccupation with sexuality to a more pronounced preoccupation

with violence and death, accompanied by an erratic, extremely fluctuating influence of personal conscience.

5. Evidence of compulsive "hungers," both figurative and literal, of many sorts: oral fixations, addictions, and dependencies, as well as developmentally primitive sexual fixations and perversities.

6. A blurring of boundaries between self and others, an inability to separate or individuate from one's parents, or a fear of abandonment should one choose to express individual preferences, needs, or desires over against those of significant others; a chameleon-like personality that seemingly changes to blend into one's surroundings.

7. A tendency to act out one's feelings instead of talking them out.

8. An unusual preoccupation with oneself in terms of grandiose fantasies, self-images, and expectations; a need to idealize oneself and others, coupled with a seemingly contradictory but equally powerful self-loathing, lack of self-esteem, and harsh devaluation of idealized others.

These are among the experiences that link the selves of those represented by various statistics of youthful devastation, young people otherwise separated by symptom, gender, social class, language, race, or faith. They are, of course, mirror images of many in the adult culture as well.

If pastoral care specialists assume that what is distinctive about their approach to the troubled self has something to do with their theological traditions and disciplines—and even more pointedly, with the events surrounding the life, death, and resurrection of Jesus of Nazareth—then it becomes incumbent upon us to discern what those traditions, disciplines, and events are expressing about the life of the self. This is no small assignment, given the expansive and conflicting range of theological voices and perspectives, coupled with theologians' apparent aversion to exploring, at least by means of theological discourse, the vast inner cosmos of the self. Yet even as crucial theological themes can be read between the lines of much psychological theory, so too can subtle psychologies of the self be discerned in current theological explorations of the external cosmos.

The present study contributes to a more explicit, psychologically informed theology of the adolescent self, emerging from the critical convergence of a sustained focus on eschatology within contemporary theology, notable developments within depth psychology, and a diligent pilgrimage through case studies of very troubled youth. The result is what we shall call the "eschatological self."

Eschatology in Recent Theology

In the post-Enlightenment world, historical and scientific methods have tended to legitimize only that knowledge which could be verified by historical analogies or by controlled and repeatable experimentation. From this perspective, judgments of relative truth or falsity were made on the basis of similarities between present and past experience or the commonalities of events. But this view of science and history, for its many dramatic contributions to modern knowledge, effectively masked other possible understandings, impeding recognition of what was new in nature or history. Empirical methods disallowed central tenets of Christian faith, such as the resurrection of Jesus or the understanding of the earth as God's delicate creation; the more bitter technological fruits of analogical knowing led further to threaten the very survival of the earth and human species as well. Modern knowledge became knowledge for the sake of domination, for the prediction and control of nature often at the expense of nature, and, finally, humanity as well. "Progress," claims eschatological theologian Jürgen Moltmann, is no longer the hope of modern persons but the fate to which they feel condemned.[1]

However, Christian faith confers its unique power and identity not merely from past events and categories, but from future expectations, most vividly witnessed in the resurrection of Jesus of Nazareth from the dead. In this event, the "future" of God's reign broke into the early disciples' lives with overwhelming surprise, requiring a radical reorientation in understanding their personal and collective pasts, as well as in their experience and action in the present. The promise of a particular future that was clearly not yet—that of the reign of God in a world where death through Christ is decisively overcome—shattered their essential understanding of self, world, and God. This startling future created, or re-created, the disciples' very selves.

In its systematization, the doctrine of eschatology eventually lost its promising beginnings as the passionate heart of the first disciples' faith. When Christ failed to return in glory according to the expectations of the early church, eschatology gradually became something of a theological relic. Distanced from its intense origins, the doctrine came to be associated with the study of the last things, the end of the world, the return of Christ, and the final judgment.

In recent decades, ecumenical theologians such as Jürgen Moltmann have begun to usher eschatology from its lowly berth as the last of doctrines to a more exalted status at the very center of Christian understanding and life. It has come now to be recognized as the doctrine of Christian hope in the present, the study of that which makes for hope. As such, eschatology has vital implications for our study of the adolescent self, given the hopelessness that pervades so many present youthful dilemmas. The hope of eschatology is not an escapist or apocalyptic wishful thinking divorced from the serious predicaments of modern persons and societies. It is, rather, hope grounded in the ravages of history, yet history perceived from the particular vantage of the triumphant advent of God in Jesus Christ.

Christ's resurrection stands in a tradition based not on past horizons but on prophetic expectations, on a God who not only has come but promises to be coming still. The resurrection demands a broadening of our understanding of future from what is merely a projection forward in time of past and present historical or evolutionary patterns, that is, future as a series of developmental milestones, economic or political forecasts, or scientific predictions. To these, rather, the resurrection adds a sense of future as that which is astonishingly new and unexpected, coming toward us from some point beyond ourselves or our previous self-understandings.

Moltmann distinguishes these two understandings of the future by means of two Latin terms: the future as *futurum*, the projecting forward in time what we already know in the present, that which likely "will be"; and as *adventus*, the breaking in of that which is coming, never completely inherent in the past or present. Future as *futurum* or becoming "offers a reason and occasion for development and planning, prediction and programmes; but not for enduring hope." Future as *adventus* or coming means the advent or adventure of something new, some event that could in no way develop out of past or present, the foundation of Christian hope. Moltmann dares assert that God's essential nature is in God's *coming*, not in God's *becoming*.[2]

This is not to say that eschatological hope consists in a laissez-faire waiting for cosmic intervention in the compelling problems of the day. To the contrary, eschatology encompasses *both futurum* and *adventus*. Christian hope demands constant grounding in one's historical context and human relationships, not ethereal speculation on eternal possibilities. It is not ahistorical or irrational. The "new" in Christianity is striking, rather, in that it begins at a particular historical point, that is, "under Pontius Pilate."[3] Moltmann notes that

> Christian eschatology does not speak of the future as such. It sets out from a definite reality in history and announces the future of that reality, its future possibilities and its power over the future. Christian eschatology speaks of Jesus Christ and *his* future. . . . Hence the question whether all statements about the future are grounded in the person and history of Jesus Christ provides it with the touchstone by which to distinguish the spirit of eschatology from that of utopia.[4]

When Christian eschatology loses its grounding in the history of the crucified Jesus, it comes to neglect human need and suffering, to maintain the often tyrannical status quo, and to contribute to the destruction of the natural earth. Christian eschatology established upon Christ's death and resurrection, on the other hand, provides for the possibility of hopeful entrance into extreme negations of human life—those of evil, sin, sickness, injustice, and death. The absence or the loss of such hope, in hopeless despair, likewise palpably impacts the historical present, leading to consequences that include apathy and psychic numbing, growing indifference toward self and others, and inward collapse and death.

What is intriguing, then, about eschatology in relation to the self is its notion that human identity is more powerfully tied to what is not yet—what is future, what is hoped for, what is coming—than to what is past or even present. Eschatological events challenge us to consider that we are not yet ourselves, that we do not fully contain ourselves or our true nature.[5] The self, instead, paradoxically awaits itself.

Anticipating the Eschatological Self

We are shaped by our pasts. For modern persons immersed in a psychological milieu, it is by now self-evident that the influence of parents, siblings, teachers, peers, circumstances of birth and early childhood, social class and location, and countless other decisive factors and events have enormous impact on the development of the self. Developmental and self psychologies pursue these various nuances of nature and nurture, parenting styles and the socialization process, seeking to render them intelligible.

While human development clearly is shaped by formative events from the past, other influential vectors may be less obvious. Is it possible, we wonder, that a person might be uniquely molded not only by decisive circumstances from prior experience, but also from the formative influences of that person's future, from what has not yet been experienced? Might one's future actually *create* one's present and past experiences?

This notion initially strikes us as quite contrary to common sense, an entrance into a bizarre, through-the-looking-glass world. How could something that has not yet even happened in any way affect what is already past? Yet the doctrine of eschatology bids us enter precisely such a realm, a world in which not everything is as it appears. In this sphere, the human self is no longer inevitably a prisoner of its developmental past, although the impact of the past is not denied. The self is also the creative product of the surprising in-breaking of some promised future delivered to it from outside its present circumstances or arena of control.

From this perspective, the self is something beyond or outside itself, external and objective, as well as internal and subjective. The self is at once "already" but also "not yet," present in historical time but also coming from eternity. The "true" or "real" self is not something one merely carries along into the future, not some prior, pristine, inner kernel of a self housed somewhere inside the body, now encrusted with accumulated layers of damaging social conventions or externally imposed "false" selves. The self, rather, is conceived eschatologically as *coming* to oneself from the future, lying somehow "in front of" a person's present reality, beyond even the negations of human life. This self becomes a *promise* of sorts, drawing one to oneself, somehow beyond and simultaneously, mysteriously, within oneself.

Could one's self be thus curiously lodged, in part, within another, an Other? To say that one is *in* Christ, as Christians commonly claim, would indicate a self somehow centered in another and open to the advent of unprecedented novelty. "The person who is 'in Christ,'" Moltmann writes, "is already here and now 'a new creation.'"[6] Such a self would be capable of experiencing surprising reversals of even previously rigid qualities or developmentally entrenched patterns. Eschatologically, the self would be one we hope to recognize, welcome, and receive rather than solely one we strive to actualize or achieve. The familiar expressions "I just came to myself" or "I came to my senses" could then be understood anew, even literally, since "I" am not yet identified or identical with "myself" or "my senses." I am, rather, *in* Christ, an eschatological promise that contradicts my present reality:

> The man who is the recipient of this revelation of God in promise is identified, as what he is—and at the same time differentiated, as what he will be. He comes "to himself"—but in hope, for he is not yet freed from contradiction and death. He finds the way of life—but hidden in the promised future of Christ that has not yet appeared. Thus the believer becomes essentially one who hopes. He is still future to "himself" and is promised to himself. His future depends utterly and entirely on the outcome of the risen Lord's course, for he has staked his future on the future of Christ. . . . The event of promise does not yet bring him to the haven of identity, but involves him in the tensions and differentiations of hope, of mission and of self-emptying.[7]

Grounded in the historical data of my past and present circumstances, I am not yet myself, although every now and then, in surprising if infrequent moments of great ecstasy or sorrow, I come to myself.

If, then, as we are claiming here, the self's consummate identity hinges upon the particular promise instituted by the resurrection of Jesus from the dead, it follows that such identity can never be secure without eschatological corroboration of the claims of Christ, without the return of Christ in glory, a validation that has not yet occurred. Yet despite this lack of final confirmation of the promises of God, devastating fragmentation of the self is not inevitable in the interim. Instead, the anticipated coming of one's eschatological self in the awaited coming of Christ is recognized and welcomed by one's becoming or embodied present self, which develops through receiving, making, and keeping everyday human promises.

Keeping Promises

Given that we are not yet identical with ourselves and that contradictions occur at every level of human experience—in our biological, cultural, historical, and spiritual lives—balancing various conflicting forces upon and within the self requires continual, sometimes excruciating negotiation. The particular claims most pressing upon an individual or community at any given moment are in constant flux. Lacking any rigid center, we become dependable persons who approximate a sense of identity especially through our *promises*. Moltmann maintains that

> [i]n his promise, a person commits himself . . . and makes himself someone who can be appealed to. . . . It is in the historical link between promise and fulfillment of the promise that a person acquires his continuity. And it is only through this continuity that he finds his lived identity. If he remains true to his promise, he remains true to himself. If he breaks his promise, he is untrue to himself.[8]

Even as God has come to be known to us through the content of and faithfulness to God's promises, so too do persons come to a proximate sense of self through the content of and faithfulness to their promises.

Promises are thus at once received by and also constitutive of the self, opening the possibility of some new future, in turn becoming the foundation for hope in the present. This hope decisively shapes present experience and becomes a clarifying lens through which one continually reviews and revises the past. While in one sense what is done in the past can never be undone, it is also paradoxically the case that what is done in the past is always being undone, always open to revisiting and revision. "It's never too late to have a happy childhood," in the words of an intriguing epigraph from a recent psychotherapy text, a counterintuitive claim that makes perfect sense eschatologically.[9] It is in such a spirit that we may say, from the perspective of the eschatological self, that the future creates the past.[10]

The eschatological self, then, is a theological way of expressing the self's experience of newness, surprise, and hope, the sense that one's self is determined not solely by past childhood events, nor is it exclusively the product of one's own careful planning or prediction. One becomes oneself or, better, *comes* to oneself, from the future as well as the past, from the self that is penultimately lodged, in part, *in* others, ultimately *in* Christ, a self actually being delivered from some future beyond one's power to control. A young child receives portions or particles of self from his or her parents, who hold that child's self in trust until he or she is developmentally capable of receiving ever more of it. In analogous fashion a person receives the self from God, coming gradually to discover or recognize more of his or her self in Christ, at first only partially in faint outline, but eventually, with God, "face to face" (1 Cor. 13:12). Or, as the writer of Colossians says,

> " . . . for you have died, and your life is hidden with Christ in God. When Christ who is your life is revealed, then you also will be revealed with him in glory." (Col. 3:3–4)

The eschatological self holds in often agonizing tension one's experience of time as past, present, and future—as memory and expectation, as promises made, fulfilled, or broken. It is a self that cannot deny the enormous impact and influence of its childhood past on its dilemmas of the present; the self that acknowledges the necessity for careful preparation, planning, and control; the self of keen interest to developmental psychologists. But it is a self equally open to future surprise, refusing to relinquish hope for that new thing breaking in from out of the blue, that newness of self received from others or Other. Not utopian or escapist, unwilling to deny its anxiety or shut its eyes to danger, the eschatological self nevertheless cherishes hope in the midst of the chaos; it is the self that remembers and hopes. If theology has too long neglected the tremendous impact of early childhood development on personal formation, psychology has not given their due to sudden, unexpected, singular transformations, what from a perspective of faith might be called the advent of God's startling future.

Eschatology and Adolescence

What does all this mean in terms of our pastoral work with troubled young people? The self incapable of sustaining tension between past and future, between becoming oneself and coming to oneself, will evince certain rather predictable distortions. The self collapsed into its past becomes awash in apathetic despair or, in the words of psychologists we will be considering here, "abandonment depression" or "pathological narcissism." Here the young person experiences estrangement from any future experienced as coming and from eschatological time, and becomes resigned to hopeless, childish dependency. The self precociously propelled into its future, on the other hand, in utopian escapism or apocalyptic desecration of self or others, negligent of its historical embeddedness or embodiment, experiences alienation from any future as becoming, that is, alienation from chronological or developmental time. Here, the adolescent abandons careful preparation, necessary planning, and self-control. More typically, disturbances of the eschatological self lead the young person to dramatic oscillation between these extremes.

Symptomatically, these distortions may be manifest in any number of expressions, from alcohol or drug dependency to anorexia nervosa, a plethora of traumatic struggles around intimacy and sexuality, perversions and promiscuity, or difficulty surrounding the processes of leaving home. At the core of each is some grave misconstrual of time and future.

This conceptualization of the eschatological self, particularly the significance of its *adventus* or coming for pastoral work with troubled adolescents, is further explored beginning in chapter 6 and continuing through to the end of the book. We first concentrate on the eschatological self's developmental aspects, its *futurum* or becoming, by considering the influences of two branches of depth psychology known as developmental object relations theory, here represented by the writings of James F. Masterson, and self psychology, the controversial innovation of Heinz Kohut. These theorists speculate extensively on our concerns for the developing self's experiences of time and boundaries, often examining them in near microscopic detail. Through empathic immersion into the lives of suffering persons, Masterson and Kohut provide a necessary psychological foundation for our present efforts to further discern the mysteries of the eschatological self.

PART I

Becoming Oneself:
Youth in Developmental Perspective

Chapter Two

Object Relations Theory and the Borderline Self

Abandonment depression is actually an umbrella term beneath which ride the Six Horsemen of the Psychic Apocalypse: Depression, Panic, Rage, Guilt, Helplessness (hopelessness), and Emptiness (void). Like the Four Horsemen of the Bible—Conquest, War, Famine, and Death—they wreak havoc across the psychic landscape leaving pain and terror in their wake.[1]

—*James F. Masterson*

Developmental object relations theory and self psychology, two influential branches of recent depth psychology, provide us preliminary entrance into the workings of the eschatological self in young people, particularly concerning the self's gradual emergence or becoming over time, or what we are calling its *futurum*. We consider first the contributions of James F. Masterson, a developmental theorist recognized for his research on youths suffering from what the psychiatric community has called the borderline self disorder. Masterson's work in turn provides a precursory perspective in chapter 3 on the case of a troubled young man named "Stan." Chapter 4 explores the self psychology of Heinz Kohut, a psychoanalyst who gained prominence for treating so-called narcissistic disturbances, which share many features of the borderline self. Kohut's psychological approach subsequently guides our foray into the life of a youth named "John Turner," a second extended case study found in chapter 5.

Demythologizing
Adolescent Turmoil

Masterson's work emerged in psychoanalytic circles in the late 1960s as a culmination of longitudinal studies with hospitalized youth. Masterson, then an associate professor of psychiatry at Cornell University Medical College in New York City and today director of the Masterson Institute there, followed a particular group of young persons over a period of years, coming finally to challenge the validity of the then frequent psychiatric diagnosis of "adolescent turmoil."[2] This diagnosis was based on the notion that it is difficult or impossible to distinguish aberrant adolescent behavior patterns resulting from the normal turmoil of adolescence, which the young person would simply outgrow over time, from those reflecting deeper psychopathology, which would require clinical intervention in the present.

Masterson became convinced that his patients typically did not grow out of their difficulties but instead inevitably worsened as they entered young adulthood. Adolescence was for them merely one more way station in a long history of psychiatric illness. From this early research, then, Masterson began to speculate on self disorders in young people. His work gained particular influence in clarifying the nature and treatment of the borderline disorder, a previously ill-defined diagnostic classification in the spectrum of psychiatric illness on the "border" between the relatively intact neurotic self on the one hand, and the more chaotic psychotic personality on the other.

A Dilemma of Separation
and Self-Expression

At the heart of Masterson's theory lies the observation that separation from one's parents for such youth

> does not evolve as a normal developmental experience but on the contrary entails such intense feelings of abandonment that it is experienced as truly a rendezvous with death. To defend against these feelings, the Borderline patient clings to the maternal figure, thus fails to progress through the normal developmental stages of separation-individuation to autonomy.[3]

This failure of separation and individuation from the parents produces, Masterson speculates, the depleted, disparaging, borderline self.

As a depth psychologist, Masterson tends to remain enthralled more with the unconscious mind than with the external behaviors of his patients. Yet he nonetheless notes their more visible symptoms, which include clinging or aloofness in relationships, low self-esteem, hypersensitivity to rejection, and self-destructive acts with alcohol, drugs, sex, and violence.[4]

But for Masterson, these symptoms actually mask the underlying pathology. More determinative of the borderline personality are two crucial diagnostic indicators that he calls "abandonment depression," an umbrella term describing a constellation of intense feelings that we will consider further below, and a "narcissistic orally fixated ego structure," psychological shorthand indicating the individual's faulty grasp of "reality," his or her inability to tolerate frustration or to control sexual or aggressive impulses, a lack of basic trust, as well as tendencies toward either/or thinking (called here "splitting"), a denial of personal responsibility, and the projection of one's own issues onto others.[5] These phenomena, Masterson believes, result from a developmental arrest in the child's, and eventually the youth's, process of physically and emotionally separating from his or her parents.

The Psychological Birth of the Child

Developmental object relations theory examines the impact on the development of self of one's mental images of significant interpersonal relationships, especially the infant's internalization of the relationship with his or her mother or mother substitute. Elevating nurture over nature, this perspective views infants as asking primarily not "What do I have to do to get fed?" as Freudian instinct theory proposed, but rather, "What do I have to do to be seen or held or comforted?" Object relations theory submits that infants seek first not biological sustenance but instead relational sustenance, contact comfort, and interaction with others. Its theorists speculate that from birth onward infants develop intrapsychic structure—an emerging sense of a cohesive self separate from that of their parents—by means of a gradual process of differentiating internal images of self from images of external others, called here, unfortunately, "objects." Self representation comes to be distinguished from object representation in what is commonly called the separation-individuation process.

Several psychoanalytic object relations theorists have attempted to delimit distinguishable stages in this process of self/object differentiation, but Margaret Mahler's observational studies of infants, and the stages she subsequently described, are among those most widely acknowledged.[6] Masterson noticed links between Mahler's findings on the separation-individuation process of toddlers and the dilemmas of separation and self-expression of his adolescent patients and became convinced that he had lighted upon the developmental roots of the borderline self disorder.

Mahler contended that biological and psychological birth are not coincident in time. The emergence of self is a second birth, in which the infant becomes a psychologically separate person from his or her mother.

Mahler identified four stages of this process in the infant's life. It was her third stage, that of separation-individuation, burgeoning between 18 to 36 months and paralleling the child's ability to walk and thus physically separate from his or her caretaker, that captured Masterson's attention in relation to his work with troubled youth. In particular, he focused on one subphase of the separation-individuation stage, which Mahler called "rapprochement," a period of heightened anxiety from around 15 to 24 months in which the toddler's actual awareness of his or her separateness from the mother increases rapidly. In rapprochement, the mother is no longer an impersonal "home base" from whom the toddler goes on short excursions of exploration and returns for frequent "emotional refueling," but rather a person with whom the child wishes to share all of his or her newfound skills and experiences, and from whom he or she greatly desires love. In the previous subphase, the need for closeness to the mother seems to be held at bay by the infant. But in the demanding period of rapprochement, the mother's optimal emotional availability is key.

Abandonment Depression
as the Apocalypse of Self

Impressed by Mahler's observations, Masterson speculated that the abandonment depression of his adolescent patients had its roots in an arrested rapprochement subphase of separation-individuation in infancy.[7] He discovered the abandonment depression emerging in young people whose behavioral "acting out"—in forms such as drinking, use of drugs, suicide attempts, eating disorders, or reckless driving—could be controlled by the staff and in therapy in the hospital environment. When these behavioral symptoms were contained, what consistently emerged was a series of predictable and highly intense feelings in the youths, which Masterson grouped under the umbrella of abandonment depression.

He found the six feelings that composed this abandonment depression to be so powerful and extreme in holding sway over these young lives that he shunned clinical language and borrowed apocalyptic imagery to describe them. These "six horsemen of the psychic apocalypse," vying in destructiveness with the four biblical horsemen of famine, war, flood, and pestilence, included suicidal depression, homicidal rage, panic, guilt, helplessness (hopelessness), and emptiness (void). Each was present to some degree in the fragmented self of every borderline youth.[8]

These intense feelings seemed to be precipitated by situations in which the young person faced separation from familiar persons, routines, or surroundings, or in which he or she had to make significant personal decisions. Going away to camp, entering puberty, experiencing the divorce of one's parents, moving to a new or larger school, graduating from high school, choosing a career—any of these moments, which would cause a certain degree of anxiety in even the healthiest person, led to overwhelmingly intense feelings of the abandonment depression in Masterson's patients. These painful feelings in turn were defended against, in his view, by a wide variety of behavioral symptoms—initially, perhaps, mild boredom, restlessness, difficulty concentrating in school, hypochondria, or excessive sexual activity, but then intensifying to drinking or drug use, stealing, eating disorders, promiscuity, running away, reckless driving, delinquency, and others.[9] These various forms of acting out served for a time to hold the ominous feelings at bay, but at the exorbitant cost of the eclipse of the self.

This formulation led Masterson to what has become the very heart of his theory of the borderline dilemma: that the mother of the borderline person, since the time of her child's rapprochement subphase of separation-individuation, has rewarded regressive, clinging behavior while withdrawing her emotional approval for the child's attempts at separation-individuation or, better, self-expression. The mother "has unconsciously received gratification from the fact that her child remains 'tied to her apron strings,' even though she fails to give the kind of mothering [her child] needs to achieve autonomy." The fathers in almost every instance remain highly passive men, usually physically and always emotionally absent from the family's life.[10] Approval is withdrawn for separation-individuation, and mother and child remain locked in symbiotic union while, we might add, the father and child become entrenched in a pattern of ambivalent distancing or nonrelationship. The child learns to disregard inner drives for separation-individuation from mother—or again, we might add, for nurturing relatedness to father—in order to receive the emotional supplies required for survival. This, for Masterson, becomes the central borderline dilemma: the child needs parental nurture in order to grow, but if he or she grows this nurture is withdrawn, and the child faces abandonment.[11]

So the child, in effect, stops growing and in turn never completely internalizes the functions performed by his or her parents, suffering poor reality perception and constantly needing to defer to others throughout life to help sort out "the way things are." The child learns to avoid situations involving self-expression or creativity, clings or remains distant in relationships for fear either of being abandoned or engulfed, and continues to live for the moment—by the pleasure principle—seeking immediate gratification and avoiding reality. Reality is, after all, the apocalyptic deluge of the abandonment depression. Thus develops what Masterson calls the "borderline triad": self-expression leads to feelings of the abandonment depression, which in turn lead to increasingly destructive psychological and behavioral defenses against those feelings.[12]

Feminist Revisions of
Masterson's Etiological Focus

A critical digression is in order here concerning Masterson's tendency to place grievous responsibility for the emergence of pathologies of the self on the parents, and even more narrowly on the mothers, of troubled youth. Without denying the decisive impact of parenting, and particularly mothering, on a child's developing self, various critics nonetheless have challenged object relations theorists' routine failure to account for social structures that heighten maternal anxiety by simultaneously idealizing and devaluing women. Mothers often may feel compelled to initiate their adolescent daughters in particular into the culture's contradictory messages, whereby women are told to be compliant yet also to fulfill their own unique potential.[13] According to Carol Gilligan and colleagues,

> the tragedy is that this [psychoanalytic] view, according to which women have so much influence yet so little power, is believed and internalized by many women, who then see themselves as "bad" mothers if their lives and the lives of their children do not measure up to an image of perfection that is in fact impossible to achieve.[14]

Mothers struggle with how legitimately to shelter their children from the culture while allowing them freedom of access and entrance into that culture as well.

Noted psychotherapist Mary Pipher agrees with Masterson that adolescence is "the psychological equivalent of toddlerhood"[15] whereby young people move away from their parents emotionally as toddlers move away physically. But along with Gilligan, Pipher critiques tendencies like Masterson's "to blame parents, especially mothers, for their children's problems," which ultimately leads to parental paralysis: "[Parents] are so afraid of traumatizing their children that they cannot set clear and firm limits. They are so afraid of being dysfunctional that they stop functioning."[16] Pipher instead strives to achieve a more nuanced therapeutic stance between parents' concerns for their children's safety and young people's desires to ease themselves from parental oversight:

> Therapists can be most helpful when we support parental efforts to keep adolescents safe and at the same time adolescents' needs to grow and move into the larger world. We can help by teaching teenagers that they can individuate from their parents without separating from them.[17]

Contrary to Masterson, Pipher often finds the mothers of her adolescent clients heroically attempting to save their daughters from a socially entrenched depreciation of the female self, yet with diminishing influence, given the powerful sway of youthful peers, the mass media, corporate avarice, and other cultural forces.[18]

Social psychologist Janet Liebman Jacobs, like Pipher, respects the analytical and therapeutic contributions of object relations theory. But she, too, persuasively repositions its etiological focus:

> Child development, as it is understood within a feminist framework of object relations theory, is not based on the adequacies or inadequacies of the mother, but on a structural arrangement of family relations that locates the mother in a central position with regard to the affective realm of personality formation. At issue, then, is not the quality of bonding *per se* but the structural conditions that define emotional development as exclusively the mother's province—conditions that legitimize mother-blaming.[19]

For Jacobs, the culture itself, and not merely mothers, must be called to account for widespread anxiety and hopelessness among its youth.

Challenges such as these address untenable emotional quandaries placed upon parents, especially mothers, by depth psychology, reminding us that, however significant the parents' formative role, neither they nor their children live in a social vacuum. For his part, Masterson largely defends his concentration on the mother, although he acknowledges that there may be "a variety of reasons," some presumably cultural, for her emotional unavailability. He also hints that the child's own "nature" may come to bear on self pathology; yet his only examples of the nature side of the equation are cryptic, such as "minimal brain damage or developmental lags or disharmonies." After mentioning these he quickly reverts to his focus on the mother.[20]

More satisfying is Masterson's exploration of the question of blame and responsibility in the context of the "talionic impulse," that is, the Hebrew scripture's "eye for an eye and a tooth for a tooth." He concludes that the adult cannot use his or her past as an excuse for avoiding responsibility for the present, but also that present circumstances would likely not have occurred without the tortures of the past: "Terrible tragedies are inflicted on many children during their early developmental years which plant time bombs that go off later in life. Even though the child had no control over planting them, when he grows up, he has to take responsibility for its effects."[21]

In slighting broad, social forces, Masterson's speculations on the origins of self pathology beg critiques such as those framed by Gilligan, Pipher, and Jacobs. Despite his limited etiological imagination, however, Masterson's clinical appraisal of what has become for many youth an increasingly fierce and complex battle between their desire to be loved—whether by parents, peers, or the wider culture—and their desire to be authentic selves remains compelling. His original and continuing contribution to a contemporary understanding of the youthful self consists in his discerning this apparently apocalyptic struggle and the accompanying threat of the abandonment depression.

"Splitting" as Primary Defense
against Abandonment

At the vanguard of the self's defenses against the ruinous feelings of the abandonment depression, and in addition to various forms of behavioral acting out, is a mechanism known as "splitting." In Masterson's theory splitting describes an emotional process whereby intense contradictory feelings are separated from each other in one's consciousness. Feelings of love and hate toward oneself or another, for example, remain unintegrated and unable to influence, balance, or neutralize one another in the borderline person. The complexity of self and others, as persons consisting of both good and bad qualities or of rewarding and frustrating tendencies, is denied.[22]

Unlike the comparatively sophisticated psychological defense of repression—a type of forgetting of painful thoughts, feelings, or experiences by those who already possess a relatively stable and cohesive sense of self—the defense of splitting in the more compromised self of the borderline person involves a radical alternation between two extreme or caricatured selves, with neither self fully determining one's identity. Psychologist Morris N. Eagle elaborates:

> The person employing splitting is all-loving and idealizing on one occasion and all-hating and denigrating on another. The clinical descriptions would be similar to multiple personalities or fugue states were it not for the fact that while the person is in state 1 (the all-loving state), he *remembers* many of the cognitions and affects of state 2 (the all-hating state).[23]

Masterson similarly maintains that a person who unconsciously employs this splitting defense

> will go through life relating to people as parts—either positive or negative—rather than whole entities. He will be unable to maintain consistent commitment in relationships when he is frustrated or angry; and he will have difficulty evoking the image of the loved one when that person is not physically present. . . .
>
> Similarly, he will never create a single unified self-concept that he recognizes as himself in both good and bad aspects. Instead, he will continue to see a "good" self that engages in immature, clinging, passive, unassertive behavior and a "bad" self that wants to grow, assert itself, be active and independent.[24]

Splitting involves not so much a "falling apart" but rather, in the words of psychologist Paul Pruyser, a cognitive activity of "disjoining by hyperselectivity" within a person developmentally incapable of reconciling extreme and conflicting experiences of reward and aggression. This emotional process is thought eventually to harden, then, into a consistent lack of tolerance for ambivalence, anxiety, and ambiguity within the borderline youth.[25]

Five Clinical Characteristics
of the Borderline Self

Because in the developmental period just prior to puberty all children face a second major separation experience from their parents, in some young people this factor alone precipitates the appearance of the borderline syndrome. The biological changes of puberty, along with increasing social pressures for separation from the parents, demand of the young person increasing fortification of previous childhood defenses against the abandonment depression. The stakes are raised, new defenses are required, and the acting out, or in many cases the acting "in," becomes increasingly destructive, even deadly. Additionally, beyond the normal physiological and social stressors at the onset of puberty, in many cases an actual environmental separation experience also occurs, exacerbating the feelings of abandonment beyond the capacity of previous defenses.

Masterson identifies five clinical characteristics evident in all borderline patients, regardless of the behavioral symptoms. First, as already noted, the presenting symptom usually involves some type of destructive acting out. The internal conflict is externalized by the young person and its tension discharged in the environment.

Second, there is typically some environmental separation experience, often quite hidden: death or divorce are obvious, but a grandparent becoming ill, a brother or sister leaving for college, or a move to a new city or school, for example, are more subtle. Neither the youth nor the family members are aware of the significance of the separation experience for the young person.

Third, there is a past history of what Masterson calls the "narcissistic orally fixated character structure," involving prolonged dependency or passivity, poor frustration tolerance, impulse control, or reality perception. The counselor seeks evidence of symptoms throughout the young person's childhood, from disciplinary problems to difficulty with peer relationships, enuresis, asthma, ulcers, obesity, and so on.

Fourth, typically the mothers, but in some cases the fathers, are themselves equally terrorized by abandonment depression, and perceive their children as parents, peers, or objects, clinging to them to protect against their own fears of separation. The fathers, we have noted, tend to be passive men, largely absent from the parenting process.

Fifth, the pattern of family communication involves acts, not words. The young person learns to express his or her need for help through acts as well. The act that finally brings the youth in for treatment is usually the last of a long series of misbehaviors by which he or she attempted to break the "vacuum of unawareness and/or indifference of the parents."[26]

Counseling with the
Borderline Adolescent

Masterson acknowledges that counseling a young person with a compromised self is a tedious and fragile process, especially in the long, early, testing stage. Such youths typically require an initial hospitalization to limit their acting out defenses, especially illicit drug use prevalent in the great majority of borderline adolescent cases. Outpatient treatment is possible, Masterson concedes, but only if the youth can control the defensive behaviors and sustain the painful emergence of the abandonment depression.

The caregiver first attempts to render as alien the destructive defenses that previously had soothed and protected the young person, thereby allowing emergence of the very feelings that terrorized him or her throughout childhood. Controlling such defenses, of course, is no small task, for however noxious to the life of the self they may seem to an outside observer, to one with a fragmented self they are felt to be a last hold on life itself. To the youth, these defenses are life, while the authentic feelings of the abandonment depression are experienced as death. To the caregiver, the defenses are death, and the feelings of abandonment the only path to life.

Because the conscious self is pathologically allied with the destructive defense—the anorexic youth, for example, feels good while self-destructing—the first task of therapy becomes one of confronting the young person with the destructiveness of his or her behavior. The purpose of confrontation is to introduce conflict where none previously existed. But the kind of confrontation Masterson has in mind here is an empathic one that seeks to be attuned to the feeling state of the person, carefully linked to the youth's thoughts and feelings. It must be in the young person's interest, not an attempt to demonstrate the wisdom or authority of the therapist. And it must be quiet, firm, and consistent, not angry or argumentative. The counselor "must be able to disagree without being disagreeable."[27]

Confrontation activates the internal image of the frustrating, evil other, coupled with the image of the inadequate, bad, ugly self, along with the associated feelings of the abandonment depression. The therapist becomes the frustrating "parent" upon whom the patient may project his or her rage or other abandonment feelings. The activation of this "all-bad" image of the self with its corresponding "all-frustrating" image of the other, if the acting out defenses are effectively blocked, consequently triggers the cling-ing passivity of the compliant, "all-good" part of the self seeking to enlist the nurture of the "all-rewarding" other. Since these latter images of self and other are as distorted as the former ones, they, too, demand the con-frontative interpretation of the caregiver.

Thus a circular process ensues: the counselor provides empathic but confrontative reality clarification; the young person experiences and begins to work through the painful abandonment feelings, then offers further re-sistance to the counselor through attempts at acting out or through passive compliance, which in turn requires additional confrontation and clarifica-tion, followed by further working through, and so on. When the thera-peutic confrontation and interpretation are effective, eventually an alliance is established between the therapist's healthy self and the youth's arrested reality ego and "real" self.

Once the acting-out has been controlled and the depression has sur-faced—a difficult testing stage that often takes months or even a year or longer—the therapy enters a second, or "working through" stage. The goal here becomes the achievement of increasing emotional separation from the parental ties, while engaging in the task of mourning associated with such separation. Verbalization of feelings is encouraged in place of acting them out. Joint interviews with youth and parents are begun near the end of this stage.[28]

As the emotional energy previously used for defending the young per-son from the abandonment depression now becomes available for creative use, new interests begin to emerge—in music, art, athletics, medicine—which the caregiver seeks to support through a process Masterson calls "communicative matching." Here, the therapist confirms the validity of the youth's creative interest by sharing bits and pieces of the therapist's own, perhaps limited, knowledge of the subject. While the caregiver avoids becoming a "cheerleader," the intent is to allow the young person to find confirmation of creative interests that he or she takes the initiative to ex-plore. In addition to sharing what he knows of the topic of the patient's newfound interest, Masterson here also begins to share "lessons from life," bits of wisdom such as "The more the work fits you, the better it will work and the more you will enjoy it," or "Experiments are necessary to find out what you want," or "It takes time and experimentation to establish a good relationship," or "One has to mourn the loss of one close relationship be-fore being able to undertake another."[29]

As the immature real or reality-based self becomes strengthened through what essentially becomes this circuitous grieving process, Master-son expects to witness various signs of health emerging in the decreasingly polarized, increasingly nuanced self. Among these attributes are capacities for spontaneity, joy, vigor, and excitement; a sense that one is entitled to experiences of mastery and pleasure; the ability to identify and pursue one's unique wishes and to sense when one has coped effectively in achieving them; the capabilities of soothing one's painful feelings, sensing continuity in time, and persevering in one's commitment to a relationship or goal; expressing one's creativity; experiencing intimacy in communicating oneself fully in a close relationship, without undue anxiety about abandonment or engulfment; and the ability to be alone without feeling abandoned.[30] Evidence of the budding of such traits indicates that the counseling relationship can be drawn gradually to a close.

We have examined one developmental perspective on the tenuous process and perils of becoming oneself, having arrived at what for Masterson is his goal of assisting troubled youth to attain qualities and capacities of the real or trustworthy self. We now turn to consider the relevance of Masterson's clinical theory for a particular case involving an extended pastoral counseling relationship with an anxious young man pseudonymously named Stan.

Chapter Three

The Case of Stan

I feel like I'm losing myself.
          —Stan, to his counselor

This chapter offers momentary respite from abstract speculations on the self, by listening more directly to the experiences of a young man we shall call "Stan." We explore the case of Stan, as well as the cases of three other youth in subsequent chapters, in considerable detail in order to underscore the sometimes subtle, sometimes dramatic contours of any life of the self. If, as Carl Rogers once concluded, "what is most personal is most general,"[1] then a lingering attentiveness to the lives of even a few troubled youth may serve to magnify for us those burdens borne by countless others of their contemporaries.

The case studies further serve to exact from us a certain pastoral humility, posing agonizing and perhaps unanswerable questions concerning the intensity and recalcitrance of these youthful problems and the complexities of intervening within the immediacy of the counseling relationship. They tend to expose and overrun the limitations of our theoretical wisdom or therapeutic competence, necessitating that caregivers cling to a healing power beyond themselves and to a hope, finally, against hope.

In the present chapter, Stan clearly is struggling to become some new self, someone at once more free yet more grounded, more secure yet more adventuresome. He senses, in his own words, that he is "losing himself," yet without any certainty as to what future self he might find or become. While one could attempt to understand Stan's lost and found selves through any number of theoretical lenses, we first will consider his plight from Masterson's developmental perspective on the borderline disorder. Later, in chapter 6, we will revisit the case from the new vantage point of the eschatological self.

"I Feel Like I'm Losing Myself"

A community college professor referred Stan to a professional pastoral counseling center where I was interning. A nineteen-year-old, white, unmarried freshman, Stan had a small but athletic frame and, in our first meeting, wore a sleeveless T-shirt that exposed a large tattoo on one arm. A silver cross earring dangled from one ear. He carried a motorcycle helmet and leather jacket. When I first greeted him in the waiting room, he was studying a course textbook. He readily agreed to my request that we videotape our work together.

Initially, Stan was quite nervous. His voice wavered slightly, and there was a noticeable twitch on one side of his face throughout the session. He had come because of an increasing sense over the previous two months that he was "losing ground lately. It's kind of weird. I feel like I'm losing myself." He had lost his sense of confidence and self-esteem, had a diminishing drive toward school work, and had little motivation in any area of his life. For the previous two months, he had been having great difficulty going to sleep or sleeping soundly. But most threatening to Stan were what seemed to be quite severe anxiety or panic attacks, building in intensity over the previous two months, during which he would break out in cold sweats, begin to shake uncontrollably, and not know what was happening to him.

When asked to share some of his background, Stan quickly volunteered that he had used drugs throughout his adolescence, heavily since the ninth grade, including alcohol, marijuana, cocaine, LSD, and others. Months later, he would tell me that throughout much of his junior high and high school years his peers considered him among the lowest of the "low class" of "burnout druggies," getting "high" every day. He consequently failed to learn much academically in school, although he thought of himself as a fairly accomplished athlete.

It was a long-term, three-and-one-half-year relationship with a "straight" (drug-free) girlfriend named Jennifer that Stan credited with his emergence from drug use. Except for alcohol, Stan had not used drugs for just over one year and was now more involved with the "health scene." "She brought out the best in me," he reported of Jennifer. But she had left him suddenly about two months earlier, just a week or two before his panic attacks commenced. Stan reported that he experienced no emotion when she left him. When I pointed out the congruity in time of her leaving and the onset of the panic attacks, he was surprised to think that there may have been a connection.

Stan's parents were divorced when he was seven, after which he and his sister, Liz, two years younger, lived with their mother in a suburban ranch home outside a large Northeastern city. His father, who according to Stan was a bright man who held "at least five Master's degrees" and worked as an engineer for a large pharmaceutical corporation, was "never around" prior to the divorce. A graduate student at that time, the father would leave home before the children awoke in the morning and not return until after they were in bed at night. Stan would see his father only on Sundays, a day he remembers his father sleeping through the afternoons, demanding silence from the children. At the time of the parents' separation, the father had moved all his belongings from the house four days before Stan's mother told the children that he was gone. Neither Stan nor Liz even realized that he had left. The only feeling Stan remembered at the time of the separation was a sense of relief that he now could make noise on Sundays.

Although their contact was limited during Stan's boyhood, his father had reappeared recently in Stan's life. The father had begun exercising at an athletic club close to his ex-wife's home, where Stan still lived, and would stop in one night each week to "let" Stan make him dinner. Stan had mixed feelings about this arrangement, recalling that his father never praised him nor told him that he loved him. In fact, his father's comments usually were sarcastic, such as, "You'll never finish college." When asked how such words made him feel, Stan responded, "Nothing, really. I just laugh it off. I've come to expect it."

Stan's mother, I learned, had a predilection for taking in "roomers," including one young man named Bill who had moved in when he was eighteen and still lived there, now twenty-one, as what Stan called his mother's "adoptive son." Stan and Liz both loathed Bill, who had taken Stan's family name and apparently was highly dependent on Stan's mother for everything from securing him a job to making his meals and managing his checkbook. At times when Stan and Liz told their mother to force Bill out of the house, she would get angry and walk away. Others, too, lived in the home, including an older woman who rented a room, another high school friend of Stan's who also paid rent, and many dogs, cats, and other pets. Stan himself lived in a semiprivate basement section of the house. He had stopped paying rent to his mother when he reentered the community college but received no other financial help from his parents.

Stan had ambivalent feelings about his mother. At one point he said that he thought they had a good relationship, for she had "come through" for him at tough times in school. Yet at other times, Stan reported that his mother was a "nosy, intrusive bother." His mother and Liz got along well, but Liz did not get along with her father.

When I asked in this initial session about other traumas in Stan's life, he told of several friends who had been severely damaged by drugs. A year or so before, one friend was killed by "wrapping a car around a telephone pole" on his way to visit Stan. The accident occurred close to Stan's home, and he ran to the scene, seeing his friend dead in the car. Again Stan reported that he had "handled it pretty well," meaning, I learned, that he felt no emotion then or since regarding the death. It was about that same time, however, when Stan stopped using drugs. He also remembered a time while in high school when he offered a friend some LSD in Stan's home. The friend reacted violently to the drug, and Stan panicked and pushed him out onto his lawn, leaving him there. Stan felt some guilt about this, for the friend "has never been the same since."

I was struck in this initial interview by a number of contrasting impressions. On the one hand, Stan seemed a very pleasant, cooperative, agreeable person. I was intrigued, and slightly intimidated, by the combination of his somewhat tough, macho exterior with a surprising degree of openness. Also evident in Stan's life of extensive trauma and abandonment were an apparently erratic influence of conscience and little emotion. These tensions appeared to elude Stan's own conscious grasp yet were visible in his strong facial tic (of which he was also unaware), as well as in the lack of affect on the one hand and the recent panic attacks at night on the other, precipitated, it seemed, by the great loss of the stabilizing influence of his girlfriend, Jennifer.

At the end of this revealing first session, I pointed out that although he reported an emotional numbness, Stan's feelings seemed to be expressed in the panic attacks. I told him that part of what he might expect in our working together would be the return of more conscious feelings and that more than likely these feelings would not feel good, at least at first. I spoke of my concern that as those feelings began to emerge, he might be tempted to return to his former drug habit, but that it would be important for him to avoid drugs if he truly wanted to grow through his present dilemmas. I asked him to stop using alcohol as well for the next few months for the same reason. Stan was quite agreeable to this. I told him that he could call me at any time if he experienced the anxiety attacks or a temptation to use drugs, and he seemed genuinely comforted by this. By the end of our first session, the facial tic remained the only external evidence of anxiety.

"She Was My Foundation. Now I Feel Like I'm Suspended"

For a period of about thirteen months, I met with Stan on a weekly basis, with only a one-month interruption. Initially Stan wanted to talk primarily about the breakup with Jennifer. They had begun dating several years earlier, and they shared a sexual relationship from the second or third date. Stan looked to Jennifer to help him out of his drug crisis, as well as to believe in his considerable, but underdeveloped, academic ability. "She was my foundation," Stan said in our second meeting. "Now I feel like I'm suspended." Yet he had no awareness of any emotion, including anger, when she finally, and suddenly, left him several weeks before. When I asked Stan when he last remembered feeling anger, he recalled that he used to work out his anger on a high school soccer team but was eventually thrown off the team for fighting with a referee, even though later the referee tried to defend Stan at a school board meeting. Athletics were, it seemed, Stan's one legitimate outlet for aggressive feelings, and Jennifer likely his only release for loving feelings.

Stan's anxiety attacks disappeared quickly after our first meeting, something I had expected once he had the support of regular therapy. Yet Stan wanted to hold open the possibility of returning to the life of a "burnout druggie," because, he said, drug users were unfairly depreciated by society. However, he also feared that, should he ever resort to using drugs, he would never be able to stop again. Beyond this basic lack of trust in his ability to remain drug-free, Stan said he feared no one or nothing, including death. Such fearlessness, he said, compensated for inferior feelings that he had about himself.

His academic abilities also became evident early in our time together. He finished the first community college semester with a report card full of A's, yet he depreciated the significance of this achievement. Stan said that his mother had been angry with him for his desire to return to college, although his only alternative at the time was a job filling bottles at a local factory. I mentioned to Stan that his mother had inquired of my identity earlier in the week when I phoned Stan to change an appointment time, and I wondered if this was her usual practice. He replied that indeed it was, and then described her as "nosy" and "intrusive" in his affairs. By our fourth meeting, Stan told me that he longed for independence, wishing above all to attend a four-year college, but also knowing that his mother would not approve of his leaving home.

After six weeks, Stan's anxiety attacks returned, although less severely than before. I probed to find out what had happened during the past week, and he mentioned almost in passing that Jennifer had phoned him a couple of weeks before and that they had seen each other "as friends" a few times since. In those meetings, no word was exchanged between them concerning the nature of Jennifer's abrupt leaving, nor Stan's feelings of hurt or anger. We then tried again to explore his feelings, and this time Stan was able to identify a sense of broken trust. He did not believe she would not hurt him again and so had mixed feelings about returning to a relationship with her. On the one hand, she was the person with whom he could talk most freely; on the other, he was beginning to enjoy some of what he considered his newfound freedom. I asked him about the level of trust he felt in me, and he responded by saying he felt quite free to talk with me.

However, in the very next session, Stan's body language betrayed something to the contrary. He looked the worst that I had seen him in two months of our work together, dressed in torn and ragged clothing. He began by telling me that he had to cut this session short because he "needed to take a shower" for some unnamed event. He had dropped a summer school course that week and told me he had talked with Jennifer and learned that she mostly wanted just to be friends. This "bummed him out," he said, and he was aware of feeling depressed. A phone call from her a few days later buoyed his spirits, and the following week he went on a weekend trip with her, funded by her parents, who liked Stan. But he was very nervous about getting attached to her because he feared her leaving. I failed in this session to connect and interpret what seemed to be sudden regressions with the honest feelings that had begun to emerge in the previous weeks.

The friend abandoned by Stan during the terrifying LSD experience suddenly reappeared in Stan's life at this time, seeking to meet with him. The friend had since "got religion," as Stan put it, and stopped using drugs. Now he wanted to befriend Stan once again. But Stan was afraid of seeing him, partially fearing religion and partially his own guilt.

We talked some of religion. Stan was baptized a Presbyterian as an infant but had no other history in the church. He said that he believed all religions have something true in them, but when I asked him how he came to know that, Stan said that he really did not know, since he knew nothing about any religion. I then asked him about the silver cross that he always wore in his ear. Stan seemed pleased to talk about it and pulled another cross on a neck chain out from under his shirt. "I'll never take them off," he said, but could not articulate why they were so important to him. Initially he wore them in support of rock music groups he liked, and then quickly volunteered that he did not believe such groups were "satanic" or "antireligion."

Stan's mother became the focus of our conversation two weeks later as she, Stan, and Liz returned from a Caribbean vacation, a gift from Stan's mother for Liz's high school graduation. Stan reported that his mother "followed me around and annoyed me. It would have been better to be there with my friends." He believed that his mother had given up on him a long time ago. She had known, for example, that he was using drugs throughout adolescence but did nothing to stop it. She expected poor grades from him in school, he thought. She took pride in having an "open" house and "open" relationship with him, Stan said. She would buy beer for his junior high and high school parties, buy him condoms when he told her that he needed more (he had been in two sexually active relationships beginning at age fourteen prior to meeting Jennifer), and say nothing on occasions when she would walk downstairs through Stan's room while he was having intercourse with a girlfriend. Stan seemed to have no sense that this might be anything other than an "open" parent-child relationship or that there might be something unusual about this type of maternal involvement with a teenage son. When I pointed this out, Stan could explain that he always felt he must be especially secretive around his mother, protecting what he could from her excessive involvement. For quite some time, for example, he had been seeking to avoid talking with her about his personal matters.

On the Caribbean trip, Stan asked his mother about his childhood. He learned that his parents were having marital problems even before Liz was born. Since Liz was two years younger than Stan, the conflicts were occurring long before Stan was two years old. Stan asked her why then they had a second child, to which his mother replied, "Because we wanted to have a girl." Stan told me how "stupid" he thought it was to bring a child into the world under those circumstances, and he was able to reflect that his mother had never been able to give him a sense of the trustworthiness of life. He now feared leaving home and failing in school as much as he feared remaining in his mother's grip. He told me that if he left home and "fell on my face," he would not get a second chance. He then finally would have proven what he sensed his mother suspected, that he really is "worthless." So he continued to hold open the drug scene as an option.

The powerful feelings continued to emerge in the next session. Stan and his mother argued about a household chore that Stan was to perform when Stan told her to get live-in "son" Bill to do it. She got angry and did it herself. I pressed Stan to talk more about this adopted brother's relationship with his mother. Stan literally seemed to seethe over Bill's role in the family. He saw Bill, he said, only sometimes at night when Stan would go into the kitchen and find his mother and Bill talking there. I began with some trepidation to wonder aloud whether Bill seemed more like a weak husband than an adopted son with his mother, in Stan's view. A weak husband, he responded. I asked whether he sometimes wondered if there may be more to Bill's relationship with his mother. "Yeah, I've wondered." He had wondered, in fact, for the past two years, because he saw Bill "getting away with so much." Stan said that he would put his money on their having an affair. This clearly was a painful topic for him to discuss, and his face was twitching and shaking considerably. He admitted to feeling great tension within, and he seemed to me a powder keg ready to blow.

That we touched on such painful feelings in Stan, and that I likely failed to provide the proper interpretive support, became even more evident by the next week's session, for Stan demonstrated regressive behavior at his place of summer employment. He was almost fired from his job but later put on a long probation by the company for horseplay with another employee, who himself was fired. Stan felt no remorse for his friend. We also returned to the subject of his mother and Bill, for during the week Stan's mother had put a note on his bed telling Stan that she was proud of him and sorry he was so upset about their roomers (although, Stan told me, he was not at all upset about those roomers who, unlike Bill, paid rent), and "[her] feelings for Bill." The apparent link between Stan's acting out, this time at his place of work, with the strong feelings that were emerging concerning his mother began to come into sharper relief.

"I'll Be Dead at Forty"

During the course of the next two months of counseling, Stan spoke more of his father as well, saying that he enjoyed his father on an "intellectual" level but that he could not talk about anything personal with him. He also spoke of an older male friend who gave Stan a gift of a gun—the one Stan had used to kill his first deer—and of Stan's tendency to prefer friendships with older men rather than his peers. When pressed about this, he said that he felt he had "survived" more than his peers and could get along on a superficial level with almost everyone. He did confess, however, that he had a difficult time with persons in positions of authority, consistently rejecting those who told him what to do. Why? Because "they're powerless. They always back down when I confront them," he replied. I asked him if he was seeking some authority who would not back down on him. He agreed that he was and then suggested that God must be the ultimate authority. "But I just don't feel any of that—I don't feel God," he said. Stan also offered that he had always thought he would be dead by age forty, although he couldn't say why. He reported having had a premonition of death before two motorcycle accidents, in which he crashed after angry, reckless driving.

In the following weeks, Stan helped his sister Liz do what he himself could not—that is, leave home. He helped her move to a college dormitory some distance from home and was clearly impressed with the friendly atmosphere of her new surroundings. I sensed envy in his voice. He himself began the new school year with the goal of grades good enough to help him get into a better college and to get away from home. However, he also described a recent fear of being called on by an English teacher, afraid of "being laughed at, rejected, ignored."

After some five months or so of our work together, Stan had become quite passive in the counseling process. I found myself pressing him harder, trying to increase the stakes of his investment in the therapy. At one point, for example, I brought up the possibility that he begin attending Narcotics Anonymous in order to confront his past drug use more directly. He resisted this initiative fiercely, insisting that he no longer had a drug problem: "I don't need it, and they'd all be worse off than me." Rather than appropriately turning to explore the dynamics of our relationship at that time, however, I found myself locked into a contest of wills with Stan, which my own supervisor helped me understand later. Stan returned the next week reluctantly willing to attend N.A., but when I shared with him my new learning that perhaps I was pushing my own agenda on him, he immediately retreated from his willingness to attend. I was worried that I would be viewed by Stan as yet another authority figure who would back down when pushed. I shared this concern with Stan, and he replied that he did not think of me in that way. This was a rocky and delicate point in the relationship. After six months of working together, I gave Stan my blessing if he wanted to take a break but also suggested that there still seemed some areas in his life on which we might concentrate.

It was during this fragile time, however, that Stan shared some poignant new information from his childhood. He had come to remember that, as a boy, he consistently ignored his father's attempts at discipline and that his mother's discipline was also erratic. Sometimes she would call in sick for Stan, even when he was perfectly healthy, if for some reason he did not want to go to work or school; however, at other times she would refuse to do so. Together we came to recognize that his "survival skills" included seducing adults with his boyish charm, then crossing them with anger, violence, or flight. Stan also learned at this time that he was born with a respiratory and gastrointestinal condition requiring that he be hospitalized for several weeks after his birth. He now remembered his very limited and special diet through age twelve or so, a result of stomach and eating problems, and recalled as well his chronic bronchitis. From his earliest years, Stan often would become sick or panic in school until his mother would come in to comfort him. Strikingly, all these problems corrected themselves spontaneously as Stan entered junior high school, at the same time that the new problems of drug and alcohol dependencies emerged.

After thirty weeks of conversation, Stan wanted to stop therapy. I agreed, suggesting that he call me at the end of two months for another appointment, or sooner if he preferred. He assured me that he would, although I very much doubted that I would see him again.

The Anxiety Attacks Return

Stan surprised me by calling four weeks later. He was proud to have been accepted into a four-year college, although one still very close to home. However, he was calling because his former girlfriend Jennifer recently had phoned after a two-month silence to tell Stan that she had a new boyfriend. Stan was hurt and angered by this and decided to call me shortly thereafter. I told him that I thought feelings of hurt and anger signaled progress for him and that it was good he had called to talk them through.

After two more weeks, Stan phoned again to make another appointment, which we set for five days later. Then a second phone call from Stan awakened me in the middle of the following night. He was experiencing another panic attack. He said that he had not slept for three days. When I asked what had happened, he told me that a married, older, woman friend, a respected maternal figure with whom Stan worked at his college's day care center, had made what Stan felt to be a "pass" at him. He told her that he was not interested but was concerned that the matter would not be resolved so easily. After listening for quite some time and sensing his panic, I asked Stan what he really wanted to do. "Not see her again," he responded. Yet he was afraid that avoiding her would reinforce his old pattern of fleeing difficult situations. I suggested that in the case of a married woman approaching an unmarried man, not seeing her seemed to be an appropriate reaction. He was clearly relieved by my response and told me that he would talk with her.

We met the next day. He had been able to sleep shortly after our call and had just come from phoning the woman to break off their contact. She was in tears, which actually made Stan feel good, since it confirmed the accuracy of his "gut" feeling about her. He then recalled how many times as a child he now remembered being out of control. He sometimes would lose consciousness, for example, while beating up another boy.

In the weeks following, we continued to meet regularly. Stan wanted to discover why this older woman had such power over him. I learned that as they worked together at the day care center—a volunteer position that Stan found particularly rewarding—Stan had shared more about himself with her than with anyone else besides myself. She then began to phone him every evening and would talk for hours. Stan could not bring himself to hang up on her, even though he greatly disliked lengthy phone conversations. We sought to connect his relationship with this woman to that with his mother, who herself recently had begun to tell Stan of affairs she had prior to her divorce from his father, revelations that initially repulsed Stan but eventually interested him. He expressed feeling no affection for his mother and continued to want to hide his private life from her.

A Self-Transcending Experience

This new movement and energy in our work together continued for several weeks. One day Stan came in clearly excited to tell me about a significant experience. After a week of worrying about three exams, he had gone into his room to meditate while listening to soothing music. As he sat there, a warm sensation moved up one arm and down the other, then from his toes to his head, until his eyes popped open reflexively, and he saw a bright light. He wrote down a description of the experience and was eager to read it to me. It gave him a joyful feeling, a sense that something good was beginning to happen in his life. I asked if he thought of this as a spiritual experience. Yes, he thought that it was but did not want to try to associate it with any "organized religion." The church, he explained, is hypocritical and scandalous. He wanted to be able to put words to his experience but feared diminishing it by associating it with an established faith tradition.

Whatever the experience was, it indeed coincided with evidence that good things were happening in his life. Two weeks later Jennifer phoned to ask Stan to do something with her, "since all her other friends were on spring break." He went to her house, but this time with the urgent agenda of telling her about his anger and sense of betrayal, the first time Stan had ever directly confronted her with his feelings. He had been nervous about it at first, but once he started, "it felt great!" Jennifer heard him out, then agreed with him. They went to a party together that evening, but Stan felt for the first time that he did not need to "take care" of her there and could enjoy himself whether or not she did. Even more striking, the party that they attended was at the home of the friend Stan had abandoned following his drug overdose. He had contacted Stan a couple of weeks before, and for the first time Stan was able to meet him without guilt or anxiety. I commented on the power of Stan's great sense of liberation with Jennifer at the same time he felt freedom from his guilt for betraying his friend. Stan clearly was excited about what he was doing and feeling in his life.

However, shortly thereafter Stan began a conversation by talking about what seemed, in my view, to be excessive alcohol consumption. Although his drinking was in violation of our initial therapeutic contract, I had not previously confronted him on the drinking that I suspected had continued in his life. Stan also wondered whether his mother had an alcohol problem. I brought up the historic pattern of Stan's not wanting to experience intense feelings, and the resulting numbing through alcohol and drugs. Yet this time he could accept this confrontative material without defensiveness.

In what by this time I should have recognized as a predictable pattern, within weeks Stan wished again to quit therapy. I faltered in not verbally connecting for him this desire with the recent events of joyful growth, increased use of alcohol, confrontation by his counselor, and withdrawal. Again with my supervisor reining in my tendency to increase the therapeutic stakes with Stan, after one additional session we stopped meeting following thirteen months of work together.

"Bugged" Again

Six months later, Stan phoned for an appointment and came appearing more ragged and unkempt than I previously had seen him. His hair was long, he had not shaved for what appeared to be a week or so, and his clothes were torn. His first words were that he was beginning to be "bugged" again. The anxiety attacks had returned. He wanted to update me on what had happened in the intervening months. He had earned a perfect 4.0 grade point average in his first semester at the new four-year college during the past spring but failed to accomplish much through the summer. He twice broke his two-year abstinence from drugs, once by indulging with his despised adoptive brother Bill, and once by "getting bombed" on tequila and marijuana at a summer rock concert.

At the beginning of the current fall semester two months before our meeting, Stan allowed a woman named Stacy, a student proctor from a previous college course, to move into his room, still in his mother's house. He had admired Stacy during the course, considering her older and wiser than himself although, he learned later, she was actually younger than Stan.

Late in the spring, Stacy was rejected by her fiancé. When she saw Stan at the beginning of the fall semester, she gave him her phone number and told him exactly when to call, which he did. He went to her place for a second date knowing that he would spend the night. Then, on the third day of their new relationship, she moved into his room.

All seemed to be well for several weeks until recently, he said, when one evening Stacy told him of her promiscuous spring and summer following the breakup with her fiancé. She also told Stan of her involved previous sexual history, as well as of her turbulent family background. That night, two weeks prior to his calling me, Stan awakened from sleep with a severe panic attack: "It felt like it began with a pain in my upper back and scrambled my brain." He jumped on Stacy in bed, and she awakened and tried to hold and comfort him. He wanted to end their relationship then and there, but had not. He also reported becoming aware of a malicious rage that he felt inside but that was disguised to the world by his boyish exterior. To complicate matters further, his mother seemed to feel the competition of another woman in his life, in Stan's view, and began to offer to make Stan's meals, along with other niceties, things she had not done for him in years.

All of this information was pouring out of Stan in a new way. He then began to comment more reflectively on his having become "aware of a couple of things." First, he now remembered crying "all the time" in the fifth grade but recalled neither why he was crying nor anyone paying any attention to him when he did. Second, he felt a "lot of responsibility" for others, mostly his mother, as a teenager and believed that he shirked responsibility for himself at school because of it; he had asked to be put in an unchallenging section rather than one better suited to his intellectual ability, and no one questioned him on this. Third, he was very angry at his father for never praising him but instead always trying to show him that he was better than Stan at everything from racquetball to academics; Stan loved now to beat his father in athletic events.

I told Stan of the great sadness that I sensed in all this information—sadness expressed so poignantly in the fifth grade but long since covered over through much of his life with fits of rage, drug abuse, motorcycle accidents, sexual relationships, perfectionism, and so forth. Stan told me that he had kept putting off calling me for the past two weeks but felt very glad now that he was back.

His articulate expression of emotions and issues continued over the next weeks. He spoke again of his new memory of crying "every day" in the fifth grade. He still could not remember why, but thought that it had something to do with being left alone. He recalled early elementary years in which he would get sick in school; the nurse would call his mother, she would come in, and suddenly Stan would be fine. She came frequently to reassure and comfort him. Stan experienced a similar fear when he would go away to camp. The theme of abandonment emerged clearly for Stan in these memories. Significantly, during the previous week Stan had indirectly confronted his mother on this issue. She had been contemplating whether to take a pregnant teenager into their home, and Stan discouraged her, telling her that she made people dependent on her rather than helping them toward independence. She was open to hearing this and did not get angry as she had before.

He continued to be bothered by what felt to him to be Stacy's clinging. He encouraged her to meet with a counselor at the same center in which we were working, which she did, because she was "seeing visions and things." He wished that he could ask her to move out of his room and give him "space" yet still maintain their relationship, but he feared that she was too "weak" to hear this news. I pointed out that once again he seemed afraid of sharing his deepest feelings with others. He then began talking about calling out to his mother when he was away from home as a child, but how she did not rescue him. Then when he *was* in her presence, he would be cold to her, showing her no real affection.

I told Stan that I felt real depression in him at that point that he was not acknowledging himself. I wondered aloud whether he allowed other people to feel his depression for him, letting them do the work for his feelings. He surprised me by responding that if only he could acknowledge his deep anger and sadness, he would be set free. "Why do you hold back?" I asked. Because the women in his life are too weak to handle it, he replied. "What about with me?" I said. He wished that he could let down with me but wondered if I too would leave him or "baby" him by giving him a hug or something. Stan volunteered that he was feeling pressure mounting in the back of his neck, yet he kept his anger and sadness inside even then. By the following week, Stan had asked Stacy to leave his house. She reacted with rage and silence as he had predicted, but she left.

I continued to meet with Stan for the next two months. I was planning to take leave shortly from my position at the counseling center and was worried that it would be felt as yet another abandonment in Stan's life. I informed Stan two months prior to the actual date, with encouragement that he work with another counselor in the same center. Stan seemed understanding and willing to continue his therapy. I learned from his new counselor that Stan continued for another six months or so, and again came to a point where they mutually agreed he could benefit from another break. He remained living in his mother's house at that time, although he had constructed a wall and a door to his room, allowing him more privacy. Fifteen months after my last meeting with Stan, I contacted him to request permission to use our work together for this project. At that time, he continued to live at home and excel in school, and was considering graduate programs in counseling psychology or education. He also was coaching soccer for a team of eight-year-old boys.

The Abandonment Depression and
the Dilemmas of Self-Expression

Stan's story makes clear that he was no stranger to what Masterson called the terrifying "horsemen of the psychic apocalypse," not only at the point at which he began therapy in late adolescence but throughout his childhood years as well. Crying "every day" in fifth grade; continuing gastrointestinal problems throughout elementary school; motorcycle accidents and fights with peers to the point of momentarily losing consciousness; anxiety attacks at night and the evident facial tic by day; helplessness in assisting and later facing the friend who overdosed; his conviction that he might never be able to move out from his mother's home or that, if he did leave and then "fell on his face," he would be given no second chance; his "handling pretty well" witnessing his dead friend in the car, or feeling no emotion at the loss of his "foundation," Jennifer, as well as his cavalier denial of any fear of death: all of these signs dramatize the apocalyptic feelings—the suicidal depression, homicidal rage, panic, guilt, helplessness and hopelessness, emptiness and void—of the abandonment depression in Stan's life. His ambivalence around separating from his mother and his despair at ever connecting with his father are predominant themes in Stan's current predicament. He cannot get far, and he cannot get close.

Remarkable to the outside observer, Stan himself failed to associate consciously the onset of severe panic attacks with his sudden separation from a long and emotionally calming relationship with Jennifer. And this was not the first time Stan found himself overwhelmed by separation anxiety. We know that his parents' marriage was in grave turmoil during the months of Stan's rapprochement subphase just prior to his second birthday. We know of the passivity and absence of his father throughout the whole of Stan's life. Stan eventually remembered being overwhelmed by threats of separation in childhood, his mother frequently called in to soothe him, or his "crying every day" in school by fifth grade.

Difficulties around separation and self-expression likewise appear evident as Stan entered puberty and junior high school. What Masterson might consider Stan's previous defenses of dietary and respiratory problems, hypochondriasis, and clinging seemed to correct themselves spontaneously as he entered adolescence. But more troubling fortifications emerged in his heavy campaign of drinking and drug use. At fourteen, Stan also began what would become, until the breakup with Jennifer at nineteen, an uninterrupted period of sexual involvement, practices complacently or actively endorsed by his parents. Evidence of rage and loose destructiveness was equally apparent, from reckless driving and accidents to violent fights with peers. Clearly one can argue that Stan knew deeply within himself the threatened apocalypse of self, unconsciously strategizing throughout his life to keep the multiple threats of the abandonment depression in check.

Splitting in the Self-Experience of Stan

Masterson's concept of psychic or emotional splitting in the borderline personality also lends itself effectively to Stan's predicament. There is an all-or-nothing quality to each of Stan's significant relationships, including his relationship to himself. In his assessment of his mother, for example, she is either angry, critical, excessively vigilant and involved in his affairs, and a "nosy and intrusive bother" who makes others dependent on her and will never let him go; or she is the all-nurturing and approving mother, with whom he always has had an "open" relationship and who, in Stan's words, had "always come through" for him. Splitting is also seen in Stan's assessment of his father, whom he both idealized in terms of intellect (he "held at least five Master's degrees") and depreciated in terms of his lack of family participation, his sarcastic dismissal of Stan's academic potential, and Stan's own ability to beat him in athletic contests.

With girlfriends and the older woman at the day care center, Stan demonstrates similar evidence of splitting. Jennifer was his "foundation," his rescuer from drug abuse, yet Stan reported feeling nothing at the demise of their three-year relationship. When the student proctor, Stacy, whom Stan initially perceived as "older and wiser" than himself, turned out to be younger and also quite dependent, and when he learned of her own beleaguered and promiscuous past and her fragile psychological state, he quickly turned on her in fear, wanting her immediately out of his life. Again, in the older woman at the day care center, whom Stan viewed as an inviting and caring mother figure with whom he could share much of his life, we find yet another instance in which his attitude took an immediate about-face. In each of these relationships there exists dramatic fluctuation between idealization and devaluation of the intimate other, not unlike the fragility and oscillation of relationship that I experienced throughout the years of my work with Stan.

Neither was this lack of tolerance for ambiguity and anxiety in relationships lost in Stan's experience of self. He was the winsome and special boy—one who, in having "survived" more than most, was highly agreeable and could "get along," at least superficially, with almost everyone, while convinced that he needed no one. Adults, although preferred companions over peers, nevertheless were "powerless," always "backing down" when he confronted them. Stan likewise saw himself as superior to those who relied on twelve-step programs for support. Such attitudes reflect a certain grandiosity or sense of entitlement in Stan's appropriation of self.

Stan also battled feelings of a different sort, those of extreme inadequacy and self-depreciation. He was convinced that he could not leave home and succeed in college and certain that if he failed he would be given no second chance. Having then proven his worthlessness for all to see, and discounting his professors' high evaluations of his academic work or distrusting himself to speak openly in class for fear of playing the fool, Stan was stalked daily by abandonment depression. Thus continued his pendulum swings of inflation and depletion, the exhausting alternation and radical caricaturing of self and others.

Masterson's Theory of Therapy in Counseling Stan

Once Stan's primary defenses, first his drug use and then his relationship with Jennifer, were removed, the abandonment depression surfaced with fierce, apocalyptic force in cold sweats of panic by night and in severe facial tics and lost concentration by day. On the surface was numbing apathy, the young man who could see his dead friend in a wrecked car and feel nothing, and who believed that he himself would be dead by forty; but underneath was a volcano ready to blow, a self about to self-destruct.

On rare occasions when I dared to challenge Stan, he became resistant, preferring to express his sense of violation or threat through defenses of flight (leaving therapy) rather than fight. Masterson would likely challenge my taking so long to confront (with the exception of my initially limiting Stan's drug and alcohol use), or my favoring the role of the rewarding parent-therapist, which prolonged his clinging passivity. Yet Masterson likely would acknowledge the threat inherent in a premature emergence of the abandonment depression in an outpatient setting for a young person with a long history of drug abuse.

These factors notwithstanding, the therapist, for Masterson, must be bold enough to engage by means of empathic confrontation the internal representation of the disapproving parent, allowing the abandonment depression to surface. When, for example, I finally confronted Stan's desire to hold open the option of further drug use, telling him I believed that he had never come to terms with the destructiveness of his drug history, Masterson would not likely see the confrontation in itself as inappropriate, although he likely would criticize the apparent desperation of my confrontational style. Instead, he would argue that this confrontation necessarily triggered within Stan images of the evil or bad part of the object (the parent or therapist), along with images of the bad or ugly part of Stan's self, accompanied by the feelings of the abandonment depression. This in turn led to the resurgence of Stan's habitual defense—first resistance; then approval-seeking passivity in, for example, his eventual openness to N.A. "even though I don't feel I need it"; and finally flight from the difficult situation by threatening to stop therapy. When I interpreted to Stan what may have been happening, both by confessing my excessive zealousness in confrontation and by noting his history of fleeing when challenged by authorities or his frustration when such authorities relented, Stan genuinely became intrigued by this new understanding, although he required a month-long break from therapy nonetheless.

The clinical cycle also was evident in the short-lived emergence of Stan's joyful real or reality-based self, evident in his self-transcending experience, his mature communication with Jennifer, and his reconciliation with the friend who overdosed. This more hopeful self, however, was threatening to him, triggering Stan's historic anticipation of abandonment, against which he defended himself through excessive consumption of alcohol and again by flight from the therapeutic relationship. The events of this particular cycle were spread over several weeks, making it more difficult for me to discern and thereby interpret the pattern. The resulting break in therapy then lasted six months.

When placed side by side, Stan's predicament and Masterson's theory of the borderline self demonstrate a tight fit, each coming into sharper relief in light of the other. Yet it is unlikely that Masterson would make any claims to having completely deciphered Stan's experience and perhaps less likely that Stan would allow him any such interpretive prerogative. Without discounting the compelling insights of developmental object relations theory, we question whether Stan's admittedly extreme emotional involvement with his mother and his ambivalent distancing from his father together suffice to account for his present dilemmas. Beyond crucial dynamics of parenting, we need also to consider which prevailing currents from the broader culture have threatened the process of Stan's becoming more fully himself. Likewise we might wonder about Stan's surprising force for life through his many devastating losses, or the mysteries of transformation that became evident in our work together.

Such questions invite multiple imaginative approaches to challenging the constricting apocalypse of self and opening more hopeful eschatological horizons in youth like Stan. In chapter 6 we return to consider Stan's experience more expressly in terms of the *adventus* or startling coming of the eschatological self. But first we set forth one further foundational perspective for what we are calling the eschatological self's *futurum*, its more gradual emergence or becoming through time, that of the influential self psychology of Heinz Kohut, in conjunction with a second case study of a young man pseudonymously named John Turner.

Chapter Four

Self Psychology
and Pathological Narcissism

*[C]lassical [Freudian] analysis discovered the depression of the child in
the adult and self psychology discovered the depression of the adult in the
depths of the child.[1]*

—*Heinz Kohut*

Self psychology represents a second significant movement within current
depth psychology, largely the innovation of Heinz Kohut, a psychoanalyst
particularly noted for his competence and compassion in treating persons
suffering from narcissistic self disorders. Kohut was born in 1913 in Vienna,
Austria, the city of Freud. The son of a Jewish physician, Kohut completed
his own medical degree in Vienna. In 1940, at the age of twenty-seven, he
immigrated to the United States and was naturalized in 1945. His entire professional psychoanalytic training and career took place at the University of
Chicago Medical School and the Chicago Institute for Psychoanalysis.

Kohut expressed deep interest in wide-ranging disciplines of the humanities, including the arts, history, music, and literature. He often alluded
to these fields in his scores of articles and three major books, the last of
which was published posthumously after Kohut's death in 1981.[2]

He was schooled in classical Freudian psychoanalysis in Chicago and for
many years sought to be a faithful adherent to the doctrines of his inspira-
tional hero.[3] It was only with apparent reluctance that Kohut came to acknowledge that Freudian theory no longer seemed adequate to address the
more severe problems of the clinical population he was meeting in his psychiatric practice. He first sought to defer to Freud, suggesting that there
was room in depth psychology for both theories, depending on the type of
problem presented by the patient. It was only in his final book that Kohut
circumspectly subjugated Freudian theory to his own self psychology.
While some have tended to view Kohut's claims as extreme, and while
compromise positions between classical Freudian instinct theory and self

psychology have been attempted, the direction of Kohut's own thinking is unambiguous.[4]

The Myth of Narcissus

At stake in Kohut's debate with Freudian theory was how to help a group of patients diagnosed with a narcissistic personality disorder, a classification whose name was derived from the ancient myth of Ovid's *Metamorphoses*. Arnold Cooper retells the story of the physically beautiful youth, Narcissus,

> the object of desire among the nymphs, for whom [Narcissus] showed no interest. One nymph, Echo, loved him deeply and one day approached him and was rudely rejected. In her shame and grief she perished, fading away, leaving behind only her responsive voice. The gods, in deciding to grant the nymphs' wish for vengeance, contrived that Narcissus would also experience feelings of unreciprocated love. One day, looking into a clear mountain pool, Narcissus espied his own image and immediately fell in love, thinking he was looking at a beautiful water spirit. Unable to tear himself away from the reflection, which disappeared every time he tried to embrace it, he gradually pined away and died. When the nymphs came to bury him, he too had disappeared, leaving in place a flower.[5]

The derivative term "narcissism" came then to designate self-involved and arrogant persons who were absorbed in images of their own perfection. Like Narcissus, the narcissist was commonly thought to be incapable of loving relationships with others, to have poor differentiation of boundaries between self and others, and to yearn for little more than self-confirming reflection or "mirroring" from others.

Freud considered narcissism a normal but quickly passing phase of fascination with and stimulation of the self in early childhood development, through which the child soon moved toward more appropriate and loving "object" relationships with others. For that person so traumatized in childhood as to compel a more permanent fixation in a state of infantile narcissism, Freud offered no hope of treatment by means of psychoanalysis, since the narcissist could not establish a necessary transference relationship with the therapist.[6]

Kohut, however, rejected Freud's pitting narcissistic self-love over against a goal of love for others. He likened Freud's understanding to fluids in a chemist's U-shaped tube:

> If the level of fluid in one end rises, it sinks in the other. [For Freud], there is no love [for others] where there is a toothache; there is no pain

[in oneself] where there is passionate love. Such thought models, however, should be replaced when they cannot accommodate the data of observation. The sense of heightened self-esteem, for example, that accompanies object love demonstrates a relationship between the two . . . that does not correspond to that of the oscillations in a U-tube system.[7]

For Kohut, narcissism is not merely a passing childhood station of loving self-investment on the way to mature love for others. Narcissistic strivings have an integrity of their own throughout the whole of life, and they mature along a second line of development largely separate from the evolving human capacity to love others. In itself, Kohut argued, healthy narcissism no longer warrants disparagement in therapy and culture.

Narcissism as a Disorder
in the Regulation of Self-Esteem

Like Freud, however, Kohut did recognize that under certain circumstances narcissism fails to develop beyond its infantile forms into more mature expressions of healthy self-respect, appropriate ambitions, and noble ideals. Kohut noticed that the chief characteristic vulnerability among these pathological narcissists involved their regulation of self-esteem. They were, in Kohut's words, "extremely sensitive to failures, disappointments and slights."[8]

Patients with less intense, so-called neurotic conflicts—the comparatively healthy persons Freud most often analyzed—were likely to be struggling over guilt feelings for sexual and aggressive impulses or transgressions, with excessive concern for parental expectations and standards, fear of success, compulsions, or obsessions. Yet they possessed a firm and consistent sense of self, comprised of a well-developed conscience and belief system, clearly delineated boundaries, and a capacity for loving relationships with others. Indeed, they were troubled by what often appeared to be an excessively developed self. Their punitive consciences and entrenched value systems waged scrupulous battle with even rather ordinary sexual and aggressive impulses, making for selves under constant vigilance for transgressions of thought, word, or deed.

By the middle decades of this century, Kohut realized that he was seldom treating patients who displayed these classical neurotic symptoms. Instead, for reasons unknown to him at the time, he found himself confronted by a rather disproportionate number of patients who were not troubled by an overly scrupulous conscience but who possessed little or no conscience at all, patients lacking the very structures thought to compose the self. In Kohut's practice these patients now seemed the norm rather than the exception.

They sought treatment for vague complaints related to self-cohesion and the regulation of self-esteem. They were distressed not so much by fear of *acting* on desires that violated their internal moral code but by a much more fundamental inadequacy of *being*, by a fear of "falling apart" inside, by the threat of self-disintegration, and by wild fluctuations in self-esteem along a broad spectrum from anxious excitement to self-consciousness to severe shame and depression.[9] They struggled with deep feelings of emptiness and isolation and compensated with grandiose self-inflation or with fantasies of merging with powerfully idealized others. Equally evident were wide pendulum swings to caustic deflation of self and others. Their frantic sexual expressions served to sustain the self but were manipulative of others, characterized by exhibitionism, voyeurism, fetishes, or fantasies of violence in sexual relations. They sensed little continuity, vigor, balance, or direction in their lives and seemed only a crisis or two removed from a chaotic emotional break with reality.

From Kohut's vantage, some sort of shift clearly was occurring in the predominance of certain psychopathologies in the latter half of the twentieth century. Although he remained hesitant to speculate on possible sources for these increasingly severe disorders, he did allow himself to muse that contemporary children might suffer from an environment experienced as increasingly distant, depersonalized, and understimulating.[10]

Narcissistic Transferences: Mirror, Idealizing, and Twinship

Whatever the sources of this shift in the patient population, Kohut, unlike Freud, came to believe that patients with a fragile sense of self-cohesion could and would form a transference relationship with the therapist. But this transference was of a unique kind, what Kohut called a "narcissistic transference," its peculiarity being that it was a "relationship" experienced predominantly only by the patient.

In the transference with Freud's more stable neurotic patient, an actual relationship developed between patient and therapist. The patient considered the therapist a person separate and distinct from himself or herself, someone with opinions, beliefs, and needs in the therapist's own right. In this relationship the patient eventually would come to feel real anger and real love for the therapist, albeit, in Freud's view, anger and love displaced from the patient's childhood experience with parents.

In Kohut's patients, these intensely charged feelings for the analyst developed with peculiar speed, indeed almost immediately, often from the very first meeting, in contrast to classical transferences that, like most relationships, develop in intensity only over a more substantial period of time. This quickly developing, intensely charged transference became one key diagnostic indication for Kohut that he was working with a patient suffering from pathological narcissism. These patients would swoon over and depend upon, or conversely rage at and seek to destroy the therapist from the outset, with fervor grossly disproportionate to the depth of the relationship itself.

Kohut came to recognize that these instant, intense transference relationships fell into three distinct patterns, which served as further diagnostic criteria: either the narcissistic patient (1) demanded perfect admiration and adulation from the therapist; (2) needed to admire and adulate the therapist's "perfection" and greatness; or (3) somewhere between these extremes, sought reassurances that the therapist's beliefs and experiences were essentially the same in every way as the patient's.

Kohut called the first pattern the "mirror" transference, the second the "idealizing" transference, and the third the "twinship" or "alter ego" transference. Together they constituted the narcissistic transferences or, in later parlance, the "selfobject transferences."[11] If the therapist somehow failed to perfectly mirror the patient's greatness, or sought to dissuade the patient from extolling the therapist's greatness, or exposed the fact that the therapist did not share the patient's identical values or experiences, the patient's response, again from the very outset of the therapeutic process, was one of either intense rage or shame.

The therapist's reflexive reaction in response to such a relationship is usually quite negative, a sense of being used, abused, even bored or shamed by the demanding person. Kohut came to realize that the narcissistic person does indeed use the therapist, along with other people and objects, not with malicious intent but for the purpose of buttressing a fragmented self. The caregiver is perceived not so much as another person but as an extension of the patient's own enfeebled self and even physical body, as a narcissistic selfobject. As psychologically healthy adults become ashamed and enraged when a part of their own bodies will not respond as they want, such as following a stroke, so pathological narcissists become ashamed and enraged when the selfobject—the therapist—does not respond in the way they desire. This is the perilous nature of the narcissistic transference.[12]

Kohut acknowledged that at times even healthy persons use others as narcissistic selfobjects to shore up a sense of self and to provide soothing cohesion to life, certainly in early infancy, but also often during later periods of particular stress. Indeed, all persons gain nourishment for the self from others:

> Throughout his life a person will experience himself as a cohesive harmonious firm unit in time and space, connected with his past and pointing

meaningfully into a creative-productive future, only as long as, at each stage in his life, he experiences certain representatives of his human surroundings as joyfully responding to him, as available to him as sources of idealized strength and calmness.[13]

The problem, for Kohut, occurs when such idealization and mirroring are unavailable to the child at crucial developmental junctures and the longings that might have been assuaged and transformed into more productive narcissistic strivings are maintained instead in archaic forms into adolescence and adulthood.

The Role of Empathy

The caregiver in such encounters obviously works under adverse circumstances. Although the transference bond necessary to therapeutic work is established quickly and with highly charged emotional intensity, it is a tenuous relationship at best, with chances of therapeutic failure quite high. Kohut came to believe that the only dependable tool for strengthening this delicate bond was that of empathy. Indeed, he nearly equated therapy with empathy: "Empathy is the operation that defines the field of psychoanalysis."[14] Empathy, for Kohut, is the natural and learned ability to think and feel one's way into the inner life of another person, present to a degree even in small infants who, for example, somehow can sense the emotional state of their mothers. Empathy, like creativity, is one of the great human faculties, akin to "the capacity to identify a face in a single act of apperception":

> The similarity between the perceptual immediacy of the recognition of a face and the empathic grasp of another person's psychological state may not be only an incidental one; it may well be derived from the significant genetic fact that the small child's perceptual merging with the mother's face constitutes simultaneously its most important access to the mother's identity and to her emotional state.[15]

Empathy is one person's attempt to "experience the inner life of another while simultaneously retaining the stance of an objective observer."[16]

Kohut acknowledged that empathy is neither infallible nor instant, nor even necessarily used toward compassionate ends. He speculated, for example, that empathy as likely could be exercised in discerning the vulnerabilities of one's enemies in order thereby to destroy them. When employed therapeutically, the resulting experience of being understood by another is to the psychological life what oxygen is to the physical body. Empathy is the oxygen of the psyche, producing deep hope and joy.[17]

So, contrary to their natural inclinations, empathic caregivers allow themselves to be used as selfobject by the narcissistic person, functioning for a time only as the placid waters of Narcissus's reflecting pond for the purpose of bolstering the counselee's fragile self. How is this accomplished? Depending on the nature of the quickly developing narcissistic transference—that is, whether the counselee demands perfect admiration from the therapist (the mirror transference), idealizes the therapist's perfection (the idealizing transference), or requires that the therapist be essentially like the counselee (the twinship transference)—the empathic therapeutic response is simply one of giving the person what he or she wants. For someone demanding mirroring, the caregiver seeks to be, for quite some time, little more than an approving mirror reflecting the counselee's grandiosity. For the idealizing person, the empathic caregiver must allow herself or himself to be idealized. For the twinship counselee, empathy would involve allowing the counselee to maintain assumptions of perfect similarity with the caregiver.

But how can this be therapeutic? Would it not simply reinforce the narcissist's disorder? Kohut's response was both a "yes" and a "no." In order to explain more fully his rationale and his therapeutic response itself, we must address explicitly Kohut's psychological understandings of the self.

The Bipolar
(or Tripolar) Self

At the heart of Kohut's theory of narcissism is his conception of the bipolar self, derived from what he considered empathically gathered data concerning the nature of the narcissistic transferences. If, for example, a counselee required perfect mirroring from the caregiver in order to experience internal cohesion and harmony, Kohut speculated that the internal "structures" that serve the need for recognition or ambition in the healthy self must somehow be deficient in the counselee. So, too, Kohut thought, the person who required absorption into the perfection of an admired other in order to feel content and secure must lack those self structures that satisfy the need for powerful ideals toward which one strives.

The nature of these transferences, then, led Kohut to think of the self as a bipolar construct, pushed from one pole by ambitions and pulled from the other by ideals. Kohut likened this understanding of the self to a tension arc of electrical current passing between positively- and negatively-charged poles—a psychological "action-promoting condition" between one's ambitions and one's ideals.[18] In later writings, Kohut identified the intermediate area between these poles as that of a person's talents and skills, necessary for fulfilling one's ambitions and achieving one's ideals. He linked this transitional region of the self to the twinship transference, making the self in Kohut's final work an essentially tripolar construct:

A firm self, resulting from the optimal interactions between the child and his selfobjects, is made up of three major constituents: (1) one pole from which emanate basic strivings for power and success; (2) another pole that harbours the basic idealized goals; and (3) an intermediate area of basic talents and skills that are activated by the tension-arc that establishes itself between ambitions and ideals.[19]

Kohut speculated that these constituents of the self surface in the infant from an initially undifferentiated state of primary narcissism. As the infant comes to emerge from a state in which his or her mother is experienced only as part of the infant's "I," the infant seeks to restore the original narcissistic equilibrium by means of various strategies. The child initially attempts to bask in his or her own power and perfection, internalizing the gleam in the mother's eye through the formation of a grandiose self, whereby the child shores up vulnerability by convincing himself or herself that "I am perfect." As this first strategy eventually and inevitably fails, given the realities of the child's relatively meager size and strength, the child then seeks to shore up his or her self-esteem by identifying with a powerful selfobject or "idealizing parent image," now content to assume that "You are perfect, but I am part of you." Again, in later writings, Kohut conceived of a third archaic strategy located developmentally between the previous two, in which the child bolsters his or her fragile self by conceiving of a selfobject—often an imaginary friend—as the child's double or twin, empowering because "You are just like me." Thus emerge the three rudimentary selves in childhood development—the grandiose self, the idealized parent image, and the twinship self.

If at this early stage the parents respond with appropriate empathy to the child—to his or her needs to be idealized by the parents, to idealize the parents, and to have a special "friend"—then narcissistic equilibrium is maintained within the child. However, since parents cannot always respond with perfect empathy, this equilibrium, like that of the primary narcissism before it, is inevitably broken. For Kohut, rather than damaging the child, these empathic failures on the part of the parents, if relatively minor and nontraumatic, actually constitute the growth and maturation of the child's self. It is as if in such moments of minor empathic failure small "particles" of the parents' selves are transferred to the child, now becoming part of the child's own self structure.

Kohut calls this process "transmuting internalization," a technical term for a familiar experience whereby a child comes to assume functions such as reality testing and the regulation of self-esteem previously demanded of the parents. A child can begin to regulate her rage or shame, for example, if her father forgets to kiss her cut finger this time. As these transmuted microparticles of self accumulate within the child, the grandiose self gradually matures into the child's own ambitions and a healthy enjoyment of his or her activities and accomplishments; the archaic idealizing parent image grows into the child's creativity, wisdom, and guiding ideals and values; the twinship self develops into an effective and rewarding use of talents and skills—all of these, for Kohut, constituting components of healthy narcissism.

Traumatic Failures of Empathy

In less fortunate circumstances, however, the empathic failures are more than minor or developmentally age-appropriate. Kohut remains ambivalent about who is responsible for such failures, but the overwhelming thrust of his writings implicates the parents, although he concedes that they, too, were influenced by their own parents' failures of empathy.[20] Whatever the source, in such cases the development of healthy narcissism is arrested. The archaic forms of infantile grandiosity and exhibitionism ("I am perfect"), of clinging to images of another's absolute perfection ("You are perfect, but I am part of you"), or of assumptions of radical similarity ("You are just like me") are maintained. The person continues to require the continual sustenance of other persons, or of primitive forms of internalized selfobjects, for the psychological oxygen necessary for soothing the self—for cohesion and continuity, strength and vigor, harmony and organization. In the absence of life-sustaining empathic responsiveness, the pathological narcissist often feels depressed, hypochondriacal, or "dead," and adopts defensive strategies to ward off threat of disintegration, including head banging, compulsive masturbation, daredevil tactics, promiscuity or perversions, or imagined illnesses and excessive trips to the emergency room or physicians. The excess of unregulated narcissistic energy frequently is sexualized. A boy may be aroused, for example, by putting on his mother's underwear or in powerful fantasies of sexual violence, or a girl stimulated by engaging in dangerous sexual liaisons. The plethora of energy is often externalized in addictions or varieties of delinquency as well. It is often when, in adolescence or even well into adulthood, these defenses no longer stem the tide of narcissistic imbalance, when the propensity for shame or rage becomes so overwhelming as to lead to a crisis at home or work, that the person seeks therapeutic intervention.[21]

This juncture brings us full circle to the counselee's establishing a self-object transference with the caregiver, usually from the very first meeting, which serves immediately to restore a sense of internal cohesion and equilibrium. The narcissist's fragile grandiose, twinship, or idealizing self is pacified by the sustained mirroring of the caregiver, or by idealizing the caregiver's great wisdom and power. Over time, however, the caregiver, now a surrogate parent of sorts, also inevitably fails to sustain perfect empathy, to which the counselee predictably will respond with hypersensitive shame or rage. Yet the therapist's failures of empathy, assuming they do not constitute gross ethical violations, are actually necessary for the counselee's growth. As these failures of empathy, however apparently minute, are recognized by the caregiver and interpreted to the counselee, the deficient grandiose, twinship, or idealizing pole of the self is strengthened. The key for the caregiver throughout this process involves maintaining an optimal level of frustration in the counselee, blocking previous means of reducing the narcissistic imbalance, while providing verbal interpretation and "confessing" even petty failures of empathy.[22] The attributes of mature narcissism, which Kohut believed to include creativity, empathy, humor, wisdom, and an awareness of one's finitude, then begin to blossom.[23]

The therapeutic work reaches its phase of termination when any of the three primary defective poles of the self has been exposed and filled out, and the self has become firm enough to cease reacting to the loss of selfobjects with fragmentation, excessive shame, or uncontrollable rage. Kohut describes what such transformations of narcissism entail for the suffering person:

> An analysand's increased capacity to be reassured by a friend's wordlessly putting his arm around his shoulder, his newly obtained or rekindled ability to feel strengthened and uplifted when listening to music, his broadened sense of being in tune with the preoccupations of a group to which he belongs, his liberated ability to exhibit joyfully the products of his creativity in order to obtain the approval of a responsive selfobject audience— all these wholesome results . . . [lead to] his reliance on the security provided by the resonance he elicits from his human surroundings.[24]

None of these newfound attributes necessarily leads to increasingly fulfilling intimacy with others, but they are vital accomplishments nonetheless. Recall that, for Kohut, healthy narcissistic self-involvement is not a detrimental, but a necessary, aspect of life, not competing with but paralleling the maturation of one's loving relationships with others. He pointed to countless creative persons throughout history who, although unsuccessful in intimacy, have contributed enormously to the human artistic, literary, scientific, and spiritual endowment.[25]

Kohut affirmed, then, not as selfish, but as essential, every child's search for those who would confirm his or her inherent sense of worth and need to see acceptance mirrored in the face of another. He stressed the importance of those who would allow themselves to be idealized without shame by another, in whose calmness, infallibility, and omnipotence the child could become, if only for a time, enveloped; or the invigorating role of those who would accompany the child not as superior or subordinate, but alongside, as companion and friend. These are the three great constellations of the human self—the grandiose, idealizing, and twinship selves—seeking confirmation and transformation throughout the whole of life. The vigorous self requires acceptance, feels a part of greatness, and cherishes camaraderie. Only then, for Kohut, will we shine in our creative possibilities, enjoy good humor and laugh at our incongruities, experience empathy for others, and grow wise in the knowledge of our finitude.

Kohut's effectiveness in succeeding with narcissistically distressed patients where others previously failed likely derived from the deep compassion and respect that he afforded them. In clinical practice and in self psychological theory, Kohut saw beyond their haughty self-aggrandizement and critical indifference toward others to a more fragile and depleted self within. He carved space in depth psychology for wholesome narcissistic self-regard, and he concluded that the contemporary social environment, for reasons he could only begin to ponder, deprived too many of its citizens of the psychological oxygen necessary for its fruition. We turn now to consider one such beleaguered young person through the lens of self psychology.

Chapter Five

The Case
of John Turner

I didn't think people did that anymore.

—*John Turner, to Elijah Anderson,*
on his being helped by Anderson[1]

The story of "John Turner", an African American youth raised in an inner-city Philadelphia neighborhood, is derived not from pastoral casework but from a previously published report by Elijah Anderson on his unofficial mentoring relationship with Turner.[2] In his analysis of the case, Anderson, a professor of sociology at the University of Pennsylvania acclaimed for his patient observation of persons in their usual surroundings, focuses on the disturbing circumstances of the inner-city environment for young people, especially the inclination to interpersonal violence and lack of economic opportunity. The present chapter seeks to complement Anderson's social descriptions by considering John Turner in light of Kohut's self psychology. Chapter 6, in turn, builds upon these sociological and psychological contributions by examining the case of John Turner, along with the previous case of Stan, through the pastoral theological lens of the eschatological self.

Anderson first met John Turner one afternoon at a carryout restaurant that Anderson regularly patronized. More accurately, Anderson was met by Turner, since the young man, who bused tables and worked at other odd jobs there, first introduced himself to the rather surprised professor. Before this, Anderson had seen John there from time to time but had not paid him any special attention.

On this particular day, John stopped Anderson and asked if he might have a word with him. As John began to tell his story, Anderson asked if he might be allowed to tape-record the conversation since John's story seemed relevant to his research interests, a request to which John consented.

John indicated that he was in "deep trouble" with the law and was considering fleeing town to avoid an upcoming court appearance for charges that he had violated probation. He expected this time that the judge would send him to prison for five years. Anderson advised him of the potentially serious consequences of fleeing and encouraged him to say more.

John was a high school graduate and a former halfback for his high school football team. He was an attractive young man, around five feet, nine inches tall, 165 pounds, and, in Anderson's words, "built like a prize high school football running back." John dressed in fashionable athletic suits, designer jeans, and "expensive, clean white 'sneaks.'" Anderson writes, "In this uniform, he is a striking figure on the streets."[3]

Now twenty-one, John was the father of four children out of wedlock by three young women. He would father several more children over the next years. John reported that his own father had left the family seven years before:

> [H]e don't have much to do with us. That's between my mom and dad. That's them. I'm grown, now, and I try to help my mom as much as I can, 'cause I'm all she got. I'm her oldest son. My brother is just a baby. He got epilepsy. And my sister, she a woman, and she can only be so strong.[4]

John was known as a gang leader or runner for "running" his neighborhood. He showed Anderson several scars from knife and gunshot wounds on various parts of his body and spoke of winning fights with three and four men at a time.

"I'm Her Oldest Male Child, and She Depends on Me. I'm Her Backbone"

John was due to appear in court in less than a week for violation of probation. Approximately two years earlier, he had been seeing a young woman named "Audrey," who lived in the neighborhood of a rival group of boys. In Philadelphia, Anderson explains, young men form often extensive organizations to "protect" the territory of their streets from outsiders deemed threatening. These groups claim the young women of their neighborhoods as their possessions. When a young man from outside the neighborhood befriends or dates one of the women from the neighborhood, he must first negotiate with the rival boys' group for permission. Without such a blessing it is considered wrong, often by the women themselves, to see someone from outside.

The young woman John was dating began to be harassed by boys from her own neighborhood, and he felt compelled to respond. On this particular night, Audrey phoned to report another episode of harassment. John told Anderson that he knew there was a good chance for trouble that night, so to protect himself he put his mother's pistol in his pocket. He said that he had no intention of hurting anyone but wanted to scare them if necessary. When he neared Audrey's home, he saw police cars with lights flashing. Expecting to be stopped, John ditched the gun under a parked car prior to arriving at the scene. When the police did indeed question him, John was polite and cooperative. Then a woman indicated that she had seen John throw something under the car. John claimed responsibility for the gun and told why he had been carrying it. Although appreciative of John's honesty and cooperation, the officers arrested him nonetheless for unlawful possession of a firearm. The arresting officer later spoke on John's behalf before the judge, saying, "He's a good young man. He did what he was told, and didn't act smart."[5] The judge nevertheless sentenced John to five years' probation and a $500 fine.

This whole incident was highly confusing and frightening to John, who had no prior juvenile record or experience with the justice system:

> I went to court by myself, with the public defender. They didn't even tell me that I had to get a public defender. When I went there, the public defender was there. He was lookin' for me. When the case came and he seen me get up, he said, "Oh, you Mr. Turner." He rushed me, rushed me through. I didn't know anything about this. . . . (This was) just like taking somebody out of college and throwing them in jail and expect for them to know what to do. I didn't know what to do, man.[6]

John was assigned a black female probation officer who was about twenty-seven years old. He had no job and did not pay his fine on time, and his probation officer held him accountable for this. His mother was concerned and managed to help John get a job as a lab technician handling urine samples at her place of employment, a major pharmaceutical manufacturer. John called this the best job he ever had and said he was making about $16,000 a year. With his newfound purchasing power, his popularity rose among neighborhood peers. But his probation officer remained unimpressed and her written reports derogatory.

About one year after his initial bout with the law, John was stopped on a traffic violation. The officer's computer check showed a detainer on John for failing to pay his probation fine, and he was arrested again. He remained in jail approximately two weeks without anyone notifying his family. He went before the original judge, who asked if John was employed. When he learned of John's job, the judge told John that because of his good salary, his fine would be $1300, and said that John must spend thirteen weeks in jail.

John spent weekends in jail and was terminated from his job. He had difficulty finding other work and became demoralized. Eventually he got the job as a busboy at an Italian restaurant, where he earned around $100 per week. His employer paid him only irregularly, however, and sometimes John would have to confront his boss to receive his pay. Although he got along well enough with his boss, John found himself at odds with his white coworkers: "They would call me nigger right on the job. They were always messing with me."[7] John once fought one of these coworkers in the parking lot, and his boss reluctantly fired him. Several days later, the owner repented of his decision and asked John to come back, because he was such a good worker. However stressful the restaurant environment was for him, John wanted the job to help support his mother, sister, epileptic brother, and his children. But he still failed to pay his fine.

It was at this point that John approached Anderson in the restaurant for help. He was worried that this time the judge would send him to jail for five years. He pleaded with Anderson:

> I got to help out at home as much as I can. My mom, she don't have a boyfriend, she don't have a fiancé. I'm all she got. I'm her oldest male child, and she depends on me. I'm her backbone. . . . Now, I don't mind going to jail. I mean, I can take it. I'm a man. I'm not scared of jail. It's my family. They need me.[8]

"I Didn't Think People Did That Anymore"

Anderson considered John's story plausible and empathized with him. He contacted an attorney he knew from a prestigious law firm in downtown Philadelphia. The attorney, Leonard Segal, reached John by phone and told him not to worry about a thing, offering his services pro bono. John was skeptical but happy about this development. Because Segal himself could not be present at the hearing due to a schedule conflict, he told John to look for a female public defender whom Segal knew who would represent him in court. John was nervous about this, expecting to be disappointed by broken promises.

Anderson, too, agreed to be present in court that day but, as a result of traffic congestion, arrived at City Hall five minutes after the hearing was to begin. Anderson rushed to the courtroom, to find John and his mother standing outside. John's eyes brightened when he saw Anderson. "Hey, Eli," he said, shaking Anderson's hand. John was poorly dressed, and when Anderson inquired about this, John said that he did not want the judge to think that he had some money. John introduced Anderson to his mother, saying, "Hey, Mom, this is the professor." She was about forty-five years old and nicely dressed. She said to Anderson, "Hi, Eli. Thank you so much for what you're doing for John. His father has not done right by these kids, and I'm all alone. Thank you so much for helping us out." Anderson thought that she seemed somewhat too familiar with him but also genuinely appreciative.[9]

John pointed to a man he thought was his public defender, which surprised Anderson since Segal told them to expect a woman. Anderson introduced himself to George Bramson, a white, 35-year-old, junior attorney
associated with Segal's firm. Bramson had just got word that morning about
John's case and gave Anderson the impression that he was not pleased with
having to rearrange his schedule to be there. He kept looking at his watch.

It quickly became evident that Bramson assumed everything was John's
fault. Although Anderson disagreed, he held his tongue, not wanting to alien-
ate Bramson and compromise John's case. Bramson focused on John's failures to meet the terms of his probation, but Anderson was more sympathetic:

> I felt he was a somewhat confused young black man in trouble, and to
> some extent a victim of his circumstances. Although not entirely blame-
> less, he was a person who needed a chance and a helping hand of sup-
> port; he was like a fly stuck on flypaper, and the more he struggled to get
> off, the more stuck he seemed to become. But the lawyer's view seemed
> more hardened.[10]

Anderson's encounter with John's probation officer proved equally concerning, for she chilled to him as soon as he mentioned his association with
John. When the case was finally called, the acting judge was not the one
who originally had sentenced John. Bramson argued for a continuance until Segal could return, but the judge decided to defer the case only until the
original judge returned later that morning. Bramson was displeased for
having to further rearrange his day.

Hours later, the original judge returned and surprised John by his actions.
He complimented John on his lovely mother, dismissed Bramson's request
for a continuance, assigned John a new probation officer to whom John was
to report weekly, and told him to pay his fine on time at $100 per month. If
John would follow these rules, all would be fine, the judge assured him.
Everyone felt relieved at this outcome. Later, when Anderson occasionally
visited the restaurant where John worked, John would thank Anderson for
helping him in his time of need. Anderson was moved when John told him
how he prayed and thanked God that Anderson had come into his life and
helped him. John said, "I didn't think people did that anymore."[11]

"It's a Shame, Man.
I Ain't No Criminal, I Don't Belong There"

After a time, John became impatient with his $400 per month salary
and tense relations with coworkers at the restaurant. He looked for another job but without success. Anderson contacted Curtis Hardy on
John's behalf, "a sixty-year-old black union steward at a hospital in West

Philadelphia whom I had known for about five years." Curtis's strong work ethic propelled him from humble beginnings to his present position, in which he took great pride. Two of his three children had graduated from college.

Curtis was apprehensive about Anderson's request, saying, "I been burned too many times now." But Anderson appealed to him, telling of John's physical prowess, his eagerness to work, and how the $8.50 per hour hospital salary could make for a turning point in John's present difficulties. Curtis relented and told Anderson to instruct John to go to the union hall on the following Tuesday. Yet Anderson knew by Curtis's demeanor that he "was asking him to vouch for someone he believed to be at risk."[12]

John, in contrast, was thrilled at the prospect of a well-paying job and was punctual in following Curtis's instructions. He learned that he was to be hired within two weeks. Just one week later, however, Anderson asked after John at the restaurant only to learn that he was in jail for beating up his girlfriend. A few days later, Anderson phoned John's home to get more information and was surprised when John answered the phone. He had just got out of jail and recounted what happened:

> Well, see, this girl, the girl who's the mother of my one son, Teddy. See, I drove my girlfriend's car by her house with my other son (by another woman) with me. I parked the car down the street from her house and everything. So, I took [my son] John, Jr. . . . up to the house to see his brother, and we talk for awhile. But when I got ready to leave, she and her girlfriend followed me to the car. I got in the car and put John in. Then she threw a brick through the window. Glass was flying everywhere. My little son coulda got cut by it. So, I got out of the car and went around and slapped the shit out of her. She knew better than that. I didn't really beat her, I just slapped her. Then she went home and told her momma that I beat her up in front of her girlfriend. So then her momma got all hot and called the cops, and they came and got me. They locked me up for four days, Eli. It's a trip, Eli, you got to see that place. We got to talk about it. There were sixteen guys in one cell, all black guys. It's a shame, man. I ain't no criminal, I don't belong there. It's terrible.[13]

John's mother convinced the young woman to drop the charges, and he was released. He also told Anderson that the hospital had called and that he was to begin work the following Monday.

Anderson now began to experience some trepidation over his advocacy on John's behalf. But John started work and seemed to be quite successful under Curtis's tutelage. He passed a one-month probationary period and was very proud to be admitted into the union.

"The Best Job I Ever Had, and Don't Wanta Blow It"

Several weeks later, Anderson received a phone call from John, who said he was in trouble. He had appeared before the judge again for failure to pay his fine, and the judge was now threatening to put him in jail. Anderson met John, who was accompanied by John's half-brother Lionel, at a restaurant. The judge had given him two days to report for incarceration, telling him the best thing he could do now was to come back with some money to show good faith and perhaps avoid jail. Anderson learned that John had paid only $50 of his fine. Incredulous, given John's new salary of $8.50 an hour, Anderson asked why the fine had not been paid. John replied that he was trying to help out his mother and children, as well as put money aside for their college education. He had taken an additional $200 to the judge and told him he would try to get the remaining $1,100, which John indeed had in the bank. John said, "Eli, I don't want to go to jail. I got a real chance, now. The best job I ever had, and don't wanta blow it."[14]

At the urging of Anderson and Lionel, John took the remaining $1,100 to City Hall the next day, thinking he would avoid going to jail. Even so, John was sentenced to six months, although with the possibility of an early parole. He called Anderson from jail asking for a private attorney to help him file the requisite petitions.

Anderson contacted John's probation officer, a thirty-year-old black man who, from Anderson's perspective, seemed to alternate unpredictably between an informal, arbitrary relationship with John and one that was firm and uncompromising. In an interview with Anderson, the probation officer seemed to confirm this sense of ambivalence:

> When I first met John Turner he lied to me. He told me he was in to see me a week earlier and that we had discussed something. I caught him in a lie. He turned me off right then and there. From then on, I did not feel like going out of my way for him, and I will and do go out of my way for some others. . . .
>
> . . . [Turner is] a self-directed person, arrogant and manipulative. He thinks it's all his show. He felt he was justified in carrying the weapon, since he'd been attacked by those guys, and that he shouldn't have to pay the fine. He wanted to get by, that's all. He had a lot of opportunities to pay. I mean he could have paid something, $10, something symbolic. But he didn't pay anything. And when you see him, he's wearing gold chains and nice clothes, so he can't say he didn't have the money. . . .
>
> Toward the end, we became friends. We talked more, and once I walked his girlfriend to the train to show her how to get out of town. We talked, and he wanted to have dinner, but I said no. I didn't think we

should stretch it out. But we reached an understanding; he knew he was going to jail.[15]

After three months in jail, with the help of an attorney Anderson had arranged for him, John was allowed to leave on a work-release program. He returned to his hospital job and seemed to be working hard. But then John began to say that his coworkers—working-class, churchgoing African American men with solid families and a work ethic—had begun to give him a difficult time. Anderson believed that John's circumstances of many women and babies threatened the other workers' values and that they had taken it upon themselves to socialize John. They often publicly shamed him, cloaking their words in humor. Anderson learned, for example, that one day when the workers were making appreciative murmurs among themselves about some women passing by, Curtis said to John in the others' presence, "You'd better keep that thing in your pants. You can't take care of the ones you've got now." Everyone laughed, but John felt bad that his personal life had been thus characterized so publicly.[16]

One day, without notice, John simply did not show up for work, after which Anderson lost contact with him for over a year. Anderson learned, however, that one reason, in addition to the shaming, that may have led to John's leaving the hospital "was that his mother, to whom he was so tied, had left Philadelphia and gone South, and he needed to be able to visit her."[17]

"I Think You're Naive"

About one year later Anderson chanced to meet John on the street. John said that he was happy to see him because he had so much to tell. He revealed that he had been dealing drugs up until about two weeks ago but had finally become convinced that he did not have the heart for drug dealing, because he was not "cold and hard and uncaring" enough. Anderson reported being "taken aback" by John's behavior but did not outwardly react with shock or offense. He came to think that it was this very ambivalence that Anderson found attractive about John, "glimmers of hope" in the midst of despair, and that previously had spurred his desire to help John. Anderson confessed that by this time, much of that desire had begun

> to dissipate because he never seemed fully committed to improving himself. Having been given several opportunities, the responsibility was more and more on him to help himself; yet he did not respond to these opportunities. This caused me to be less and less interested in helping him; I became increasingly disappointed by his behavior, but I still had hope for him.[18]

For his part, too, John seemed to find Anderson similarly enigmatic, a naive professor on the one hand but a person helpful to John in times of need on the other. Anderson became convinced that John sought to keep Anderson interested in helping him by talking about his desire to go to church, wanting to be a hard worker, or saving money for his children's college education. But Anderson finally came to see this behavior, however sincere John's intentions, as a manipulative game. He did not believe that John's recent resolve to quit the drug trade would be unwavering.

At the close of this conversation, John asked Anderson if he could borrow five dollars and wondered if Anderson would help him get back his old hospital job. Anderson had no intention of involving Curtis again but told John that he would see what else was available. However, having lent John the money, Anderson did not expect to see him again soon.

Still John persisted. One week later, he phoned Anderson to ask about the job search. Anderson tried to stall him. Then, during a weekend when Anderson was out of town, John and his girlfriend came to Anderson's home and spoke with his wife. She told John that Anderson was at his office, and Anderson later found on his office answering machine many desperate messages asking where he was and pleading for a job. On Anderson's return home, as his wife was relaying this information to him, John called the house, and Anderson agreed to meet him because, he wrote, "I had by now come to realize that I had to sever my contact with him, and in order to do that I had to come up with a way to keep him from contacting me."[19]

Anderson met John and his girlfriend. Now John wanted ten dollars, which Anderson gave him. He asked John if he had thought about joining the Army. John instantly was interested. Then John surprised Anderson by asking him out of the blue if he had an extra suit. Anderson asked him why he needed a suit, to which John responded by saying that he wanted to go to church on Sunday. Anderson still believed that there was a part of John that truly wanted to reform, but he told John that he did not have a suit to give.

They met the following morning and drove to the Army recruiting station. The black sergeant's first question to John was, "Are you on probation?" to which John had to say yes. The recruiter told him to return only after that was "cleared up." After an unsuccessful attempt to meet with his probation officer, Anderson and John then went to the restaurant district. On the walk, John began to question Anderson's position. He wondered if "all that professor shit" really worked, and whether, had Anderson been a white professor, he would have had more influence with the Army recruiter. John then said, "It don't work, man. I think you're naive," which Anderson took to be "really a major development in [their] relationship, because he had never called [him] that before." They talked about this some, with John escalating his charges against Anderson for failing to get him into the Army.

Finally, Anderson reported getting "fed up," and took John into the first restaurant they came to. They asked for the manager, before whom Anderson vouched for John's solid work history in restaurants and his desire to get a job. The manager sent them back to the kitchen to talk with someone else; the two men then conferred, and the manager returned to ask John when he could start. John was elated, thinking Anderson once again to be some kind of miracle worker: "I got it, man, I got it! How'd you do that? How'd you do that?"[20]

Later that afternoon, Anderson met with John again. This time they spoke more intimately of John's quitting his job at the hospital, where Anderson learned of the shame John felt as he was teased by the other men over his girlfriends and weekend incarcerations. He also told Anderson that one of his girlfriends had "used him" to get pregnant twice and then would not allow him to see the children. He also expressed how much he missed his mother since she had moved away, how lonely Thanksgiving had been without her, and how he had enjoyed being down south with her but had to return because of the terms of his probation and his desire to care for his children.

Then, after telling all this, John asked Anderson for more money, this time $150. Anderson resisted at first but then decided after some reflection to give John the money, seeing this as his chance to sever their relationship. He knew that John's code of honor, as well as his history of not repaying past debts, would prevent him from contacting Anderson after the loan. Anderson concludes this biographical portion of their journey as follows:

> I had continued to help John even after it had become apparent that he was using me, because I wanted to see how he responded to various situations. At this point, however, I felt I had developed a rather complete picture of him, in addition to which I was beginning to feel uneasy about our association. Consistent with my expectations, I have indeed not seen him since, but I have heard of him. The street life which he found so compelling seems to have brought him to a corner in Baltimore. There he had an altercation with somebody over something, perhaps a misunderstood drug deal, and he wound up being shot in the gut. On the streets it is said that as a result of that shooting, he is "carrying around a bag" and will be for the rest of his life. He is now about 27.[21]

The Allure of the Streets

Anderson's labors in relationship with John Turner outline in dramatic fashion the tensions and complexities of life for one caught in an urban web of racism, poverty, violence, and the allure of the streets. The case depicts in one at-risk youth the potentially devastating consequences of this social vacuum devoid of empathy. It likewise exemplifies the complexities of his caregiver's laudable, but finally palliative, efforts to reverse the impairment. Like Kohut with his patients, Anderson approached John Turner with an attitude of thoughtful respect and sensitivity. His conclusions, even after being rebuffed in his efforts, remain charitable toward youths caught in John's circumstances of despair.

Anderson became convinced that at the root of the violence and malaise of African American youth in the inner city is a lack of real jobs that pay living wages. Holding little credible hope for attaining status in the conventional working world, urban youths often feel compelled to seek it in the streets, by opposing the very culture that they believe opposes them. The lure of this oppositional culture pressures even those young people who come from families that esteem conventional values—by far the vast majority of inner-city families, by Anderson's accounting—to turn to the street to fulfill aspirations for wealth and power. The resulting battle between "decent" families and those of the "street"—designations the residents themselves use—is a struggle for body and soul of their children.[22]

The so-called decent families labor to instill in their children a deeply held religious faith and mainstream work ethic, and strongly oppose drugs and teen pregnancies. The street orientation, by contrast, is marked by what Anderson considers a pathological and often violent striving for a fleeting commodity known as "respect." As centerpiece of the urban "code of the streets," respect is "viewed as almost an external entity that is hard-won but easily lost, and so must be constantly guarded."[23] On the street, even seemingly minor infractions such as maintaining eye contact too long may be viewed as "dissing" or disrespecting another's carefully engineered manhood, a transgression that can lead to life-threatening consequences. The resulting necessary vigilance in reading another's intentions by means of the code likely serves to prolong the very lives of urban residents.

Anderson considers the fundamental lesson in the story of John Turner to be that of the "basic incompatibility" between these two opposing cultures within the inner city, the conflicting values waging war for John's personal identity. By the time that Anderson met him, of course, John's street persona and skills were highly developed and, at least in his world, even salvific. He proudly displayed the physical scars of the violent skirmishes he had waged and won, heavily vested in the oppositional culture as his source of confidence.

Anderson recognized through this experience that providing jobs or social programs for poor urban youth, although a necessary obligation, is not enough. He calls in addition for a more intangible quality, likely requiring earlier childhood intervention—an inner attitude or outlook that would allow youth like John to take advantage of such opportunities when presented:

Only then can they leave behind the attitudes and behavior that block their advancement in the mainstream but that also give them security in negotiating within their world. The reality is that these young men are being written off by mainstream society, they know it, and the world is poorer for their loss.[24]

What Anderson has in mind by these requisite "personal resources" and a transformed "outlook" likely involves the very organization of John's self, which provides us occasion to build upon his conclusions by means of Kohut's self psychology.

A Relationship with a Contemporary Narcissus

The story of John Turner is a tragedy reminiscent of the myth of Narcissus. Like Narcissus, John was a physically perfect youth—"built like a prize high school football running back," in Anderson's words, and "a striking figure on the streets." Like Narcissus, John seemed largely incapable of reciprocating the love of any who desired to know him beyond a passing sexual interest. John shared with Narcissus a lack of accurate social mirrors throughout life, resulting in a limited sense of self and the larger world, coupled with a tendency to be absorbed in images of his own importance.

Also like Narcissus, John's smooth but fragile facade of self-assurance could not sustain him in his ever-accumulating predicaments. Although he did not seek therapy or a pastoral relationship, his crises escalated until he implored a complete stranger, Elijah Anderson, for assistance. Even then John disguised his desperation by claiming his true fear in going to jail was that his family would lose his support.

At face value, John's words indicate at least a rudimentary development of self, one who senses obligation to his immediate family, or perhaps senses that he should sense such obligation. While likely sincere in this perception, John was much less aware of his own deep reliance on his family, particularly his mother, for sustaining his semblance of self. John's is not a well-delineated self remorseful for having violated his own high standards and obligations but an enfeebled self confronting the abyss. His struggle was not over pangs of conscience for having transgressed the law or the terms of his probation, however unwarranted his initial conviction. He was not condemning himself for his failure to pay his fine. More apparent is someone in danger of annihilation, uncertain of where to turn, willing to cling even to a stranger in hopes of holding himself together, the fragile self of the pathological narcissist.

The intense rapport quickly established between John and Anderson likewise parallels Kohut's descriptions of the narcissistic transference. From the beginning John pours out his story with little coaxing from Anderson, pleads for his counsel, and is relieved by his willingness to intervene. Just days later, on the morning of the first court hearing, John phoned Anderson, worried that he would not be present at the hearing as promised, again demonstrating an intensity in their initial connection. This instant but unilateral bonding was gratifying to John from the outset. He was willing to wager high stakes on his relatively unknown guide.

Which of the selfobject transferences does John establish with Anderson? A case could be made for all three. One could argue, for example, in support of the twinship transference—of John's assuming that he is like Anderson, or wanting to be, seen in John's occasional desire to go to church or to save money for his children's education. Either the twinship or idealizing transferences could be invoked in assessing John's response to Anderson at the courthouse at the initial hearing. John's face lit up when Anderson arrived, and he greeted him with the words, "Hey, Eli," demonstrating both exaggerated familiarity and idealization. This informality and pride is also evident as John beams to his mother, "Hey, Mom, this is the professor." That John initially chose to introduce himself to Anderson at all indicates that he likely esteemed Anderson from afar. The idealizing transference is equally evident at times when John perceived as magical Anderson's ability to transform legal fixes and to obtain jobs for him. What from Anderson's perspective were relatively ordinary social transactions were for John extraordinary feats.

An even stronger case can be made for what Kohut considered the more developmentally regressive mirror transference. From the beginning and throughout their relationship, Anderson assumes the role of a reflective mirror, giving relatively passive but deeply attentive audience to John's feelings, needs, and desires. He was willing to listen at length to John's story and predicament. He believed and supported John at a time when the young man desperately needed both. This mirror transference likely was enhanced because Anderson felt little need to play a role of moral counselor to John. Instead Anderson assumed the role of sociologist, of imperturbable researcher or enthralled student, giving John wide tether to explore and expose what he needed without evaluation or condemnation. Anderson, at least initially, wanted to learn from rather than teach John, a dispassion that paradoxically enhanced Anderson's empathy, given the peculiar demands of the mirror transference.

He intuitively knew that John would respond to any direct confrontation with rage or flight, as indeed John reflexively reacted to shaming from others—that of his restaurant and hospital coworkers, the courts and probation officers, his former girlfriend, and his peers on the street. Anderson made space to sustain their fragile relationship by consciously withholding his own self. When chancing upon John, for example, after a year-long hiatus in their relationship, during which John had become a drug dealer, Anderson withheld his consternation at John's eager recounting of his recent past. He writes, "I was rather taken aback by his life style, and began to wonder what was going on. I did not, however, act shocked or offended, because that would have scared him off."[25] Expressions of the depth and range of Anderson's own self are disallowed here, revealing the ravenous hunger in John's deficient grandiose self for a calming "gleam" of acceptance in another's eye, or what Kohut described as the mirror transference.

The Limits of Empathy

Like other caregivers who work with narcissistically disordered persons, Anderson came to experience the significant personal cost involved in such unrequited empathy. From the beginning, Anderson offered generous support, assuring John, for example, that he would be present at his court hearing. We need not assume that Anderson's own motives for helping were entirely altruistic; he is, after all, a professional sociologist who, in his own words, "had continued to help John even after it had become apparent that he was using [him], because [Anderson] wanted to see how he responded to various situations."[26] There is ambiguity here, as in any helping scenario, in terms of who was helping whom. John also was assisting Anderson, supplying him with research data on inner-city youth. Despite this element of mutuality, it is also clear that Anderson demonstrated genuine empathy for John. He found disconcerting the reactions like those of Curtis, the hospital union supervisor, who had "been burned too many times now," or of John's probation officer, who considered John "arrogant and manipulative," one who "thinks it's all his show."[27] Anderson clearly went the extra mile for months, even years, longer than any previous outside advocate in John's life.

Eventually, doubts welled up within Anderson. He began to question his own judgment following the incident in which John was incarcerated for beating up his former girlfriend. He grew incredulous with John's refusal to pay his court fine. Then upon learning that John had begun pressuring Anderson's wife at their home, he decided to sever their ties. Anderson was exasperated by the objectification he experienced from a youthful narcissist, and their relationship finally succumbed to the seemingly insatiable possessiveness of John's grandiose self.

Many caregivers will find it easy to identify with Anderson's perhaps necessary "failure of empathy" in lending to John the $150, the act that intentionally ended their association. Even then, although discouraged, Anderson did not lose hope for John Turner or others like him. Nor would he tolerate placing all responsibility for their problems on the youth themselves. Rather, I think, Anderson would be sympathetic to Kohut's conviction that the severity of confusion in persons like John results from an environment experienced as threateningly distant. John's self was miscarried by its long-term "exposure to the coldness, the indifference of the nonhuman, the nonempathically responding world," a chilling of self familiar to far too many contemporary youth.[28]

In Search of an Alternate Ending

In this unwelcoming social milieu, the rigid and elaborate code through which residents negotiate potentially life-threatening public interactions dictates survival itself. John's proclivity to violence in reaction to shaming or being dissed, however ultimately pathological, remains in his world also normative and sustaining. We witness in him unceasing swings from rage to shame, from the self's aggrandizement to its exhaustion. He is subject to violent outbursts, demonstrated in his clashing with the racist restaurant coworker, in his "slapping" the mother of his son, or in reports of fighting four men at a time.

John also exhibits childlike vulnerability in his humiliation by Curtis and the other hospital coworkers, in his clinging to Anderson for guidance and support, in finding himself empty and shaken by his mother's move south, in the sheer depression that emerged when a long incarceration loomed imminent, and in his acknowledging discouragement at being used by a woman to father two children whom she now prevented him from seeing. Each of these poignant scenes plays out the vengeance of the gods upon a young Narcissus, whose destiny indicates the same pining into nothingness as his mythological forebear.

Must we assume then that all hope has been extinguished for John Turner and countless other youth, urban and suburban, whose lives seem similarly vacuous? Might not some ember remain even still? Very few caregivers would have the tenacity to see John through to that soothing and invigorating station in life where his deep longings for mirroring acceptance, for merging with greatness, and for finding a companion for the journey were accomplished. But what if such desires were to encounter One perfectly empathic, with longings wholly complementary, and in whose mirror image John's very self was fashioned? Who then could say whether a beautiful flower might not yet bloom at the edge of the pool?

PART II

Coming to Oneself:
Youth in Eschatological Perspective

Chapter Six

The Eschatological Self

Phenomenologically, hoping is connected with patience and forbearance. Hoping involves waiting, though with an added quality of awaiting. Wishing, on the contrary, is clearly associated with urges toward tension discharge. In its primordial form, wishing seeks immediate gratification. . . . The experience of hoping presupposes the experience of doubting, fearing and despairing. Hoping is not an elegant drifting in leisure and comfort, as a tourist may do in a Venetian gondola. It is much more like steering a ship in a gale. Hoping is a singularly unsentimental and unromantic affair. It permits no departure from reality, otherwise it becomes illusion and delusion. In Marcel's words: "Hope is a response to tragedy."[1]

—Paul W. Pruyser

We focused in Part I on the process of becoming a self in light of recent depth psychology and considered the lives of two young men whose sense of self appeared tentative and fragile, on the verge of annihilation. In Part II, we build on this developmental base by elaborating on the coming or eschatological nature of the self initially introduced in chapter 1. The theoretical interlude of the present chapter seeks to clarify the eschatological self's twin aspects of becoming and coming, by further engaging the psychological theorists and case studies of Part I with Christian eschatological theology. Chapters 7 and 8 explore the lives of two other troubled young people from this eschatological perspective, and the epilogue in turn offers concluding convictions concerning our pastoral work with youth in crisis. But first we briefly revisit the work of Masterson and Kohut.

The Stewardship of Pain

Certain theoretical and clinical distinctions exist between the therapeutic approaches of Masterson and Kohut. Masterson's theory of the borderline dilemma, for example, emphasizes the unconscious internal drama played out by the abandonment depression wreaking havoc on the self, and his clinical approach focuses on early confrontation of the patient's destructive acting-out defenses. Kohut, in contrast, concentrated on his patients' more conscious experience of self-depletion or disintegration, while clinically practicing a more leisurely empathic acceptance of their narcissistic strivings for mirroring and/or idealization.

Masterson and Kohut share key assumptions as well—most notably, that so-called borderline and narcissistic disorders can be linked to early childhood experiences in relation to parents and siblings, for which the intense therapeutic relationship serves as corrective. Both Masterson and Kohut perceive at the heart of these disorders in young people severe vicissitudes in terms of boundaries—in their inability to differentiate self from significant others as well as their deficiencies in distinguishing between a true and false self.[2] They speculate that since infancy these youth have been paralyzed by an inner contradiction or double bind: if they grow and begin seeking to express, in Masterson's words, the "real self," or attempting to solicit, in Kohut's words, appropriate empathic mirroring of healthy narcissistic strivings, they stand to lose the emotional support and encouragement, the life-sustaining psychic oxygen, needed to survive. But their ensuing avoidance of growth leads to a psychosocial death as well. A Faustian bargain is struck, whereby an emotional eclipse of self becomes the price paid for survival.

The result? Instead of a self structure that is strong yet flexible, the disordered self is rigid and brittle, easily fragmenting in times of stress. Instead of a self that, even in the midst of constant change, remains recognizable by self and others as continuous over time, the disordered self cannot negotiate tensions between its past and future: "If I grow, I will die; therefore I have no choice but to live only for the moment, for today." Instead of a self with boundaries both porous yet firm, allowing it to indwell with empathy and love the self of another, or to go out of itself into another without fusion or dissolution, the boundaries of the disordered self seem opened entirely to invasion from another, or cordoned off by shame or rage from every intimate relation with another.

In each of these areas, the difficulty lies in the inability of the young person to sustain inner tensions between self and other, between constancy and change, between past and future. Instead, these paradoxical contradictions inherent in human development are collapsed into one or the other pole in an effort to avoid suffering. Over time, of course, this unconscious refusal to suffer leads to an ever more severe and destructive suffering.

The purpose of clinical work becomes then not the elimination of all suffering but the enabling of realistic suffering, thereby countering the increasingly detrimental effects of defensive suffering. For Masterson, this process involves admitting into consciousness the terrible feelings of the abandonment depression; for Kohut, it means sustaining one's shame and rage, the narcissistic by-products of a nonempathically responding object world. Put differently, the goal is to enable the troubled youth, by means of a corrective therapeutic relationship, to abide a level of suffering inherent in the human condition, in order to combat the suffering created by a prior refusal or developmental inability to sustain it. In the intriguing expression of Frederick Buechner in an essay on adolescence, the caregiver aims to assist the young person in "the stewardship of pain":

> We are never more in touch with life than when life is painful, never more in touch with hope than we are then, if only the hope of another human presence to be with us and for us.
>
> Being a good steward of your pain involves . . . taking the risk of being open, of reaching out, of keeping in touch with the pain as well as the joy of what happens because at no time more than at a painful time do we live out of the depths of who we are instead of out of the shallows. There is no guarantee that we will find a pearl in the depths, that the end of our pain will have a happy end, or even any end at all, but at least we stand a chance of finding in those depths who we most deeply and humanly are and who each other are. . . . And that in itself is a pearl of great price. It is a way of transmuting passion into compassion, of leaving the prison of selfhood for a landscape of selves, of spinning straw into gold.[3]

Crying at the Happy Ending

This raises the question, then, of just what these young people would require in order willingly to embrace such frightening apocalyptic feelings in becoming faithful stewards of their pain. What enables someone to exchange defensive for realistic suffering necessary for transformation and healing?

In decades of compelling empirical research into such questions, a group of clinicians at the San Francisco Psychoanalytic Institute concluded that the answer, in a word, is *safety* or, allowing ourselves theological license, *hope*. In order to tolerate the emergence of such terrifying feelings into consciousness, one must first sense that certain "conditions of safety" have been satisfied. Drs. Joseph Weiss and Harold Sampson and colleagues argue that a person will not reveal dreaded impulses or desires, or reexperience threatening memories of past abuse or socially unacceptable aspects of one's conscious or unconscious self, unless it is first safe to do so.[4]

Their prototypic illustration of the conditions of safety is the familiar experience of crying at the happy ending of a movie or novel. Why, Weiss asks,

> does a person experience sadness and weep just at the moment when the happy ending should result in his being happy? It cannot be explained, in accord with early [Freudian defense] theory, as a consequence of an intensification and eruption of sadness into consciousness. For at the saddest moments, crying did not occur. Also, intensification of emotion would be accompanied by tension and anxiety, but, in fact, the crying person is not more tense nor more anxious and does not experience the sadness and crying as ego-alien. The answer . . . is that the happy ending provides the safety necessary to experience fully the sadness.[5]

We do not cry when the lovers separate but instead save our tears for the time when they are happily reunited, when it is safe to do so. The happy ending allows the viewer or reader to experience the sadness fully, to exchange pent-up sorrow or tension for realistic suffering in a satisfying release of joyful sadness. The happy ending provides hope enough to enable the emergence of previously suppressed pain:

> The grief and the impulse to cry are repressed until the situation no longer merits this reaction. Then, at the happy ending, there is no longer any need for the grief to be repressed. When the inhibition is lifted the energy that is used to maintain it is unnecessary, and may be discharged, causing pleasure and allowing for the expression of grief.[6]

Numerous examples of this phenomenon could be offered from everyday life: a child lost in a supermarket is apt to cry only after the parent has been spotted or help is on the way; the individual who has worked hard all his life to gain recognition cries only at his retirement dinner; or a mother releases her tears of anxiety and pain in childbirth only after she is safely through the delivery.[7] It applies to the counseling room or confessional as well: one can face more fully the deplorable aspects of oneself only upon sensing the safety of a happy ending in the strength, competence, or empathic acceptance of the therapist or confessor or, in theological terms, in the unmerited grace of God.[8]

Weiss assumes that psychopathology results from pathogenic beliefs that are internalized in response to traumatic experiences in infancy and that later the person struggles to disprove. Therapy becomes, then, "the process by which the patient works with the therapist at the task of disconfirming his [or her] pathogenic beliefs," initially by presenting some conscious or usually unconscious test to the therapist to determine the degree of safety.[9] For example, the therapist's response to a male patient's gift is to tactfully refuse the gift and to remind the patient of the analytic contract [i.e., gift giving is not allowed]. During the next session the patient begins to talk about homosexual fear and fantasies. The interpretation of this sequence of events is that the patient *tests* the analyst by offering him a gift, is reassured by the analyst's refusal, which is unconsciously tantamount to a communication that [the therapist] will not be seduced and therefore constitutes test-passing, and then feels that it is safe to bring forth the warded-off homosexual contents.[10]

Or similarly,

a female patient unconsciously believed that the therapist would want to criticize her accomplishments as her father had done. She tested this belief in an early session by saying that although she had laid out her problems fairly well, she was being too intellectual and was probably avoiding something. The therapist questioned the patient's self-criticism of her performance during the session. She did not reply directly but somewhat later in the session she spontaneously recalled a childhood incident. Her father had pointed out to her that a school paper about which she had felt pride had not addressed certain issues and was therefore inadequate. The patient began the next session by talking for the first time about how good she was at her research work. . . . [In this sequence of events] the patient tested her pathogenic belief first by inviting the therapist to agree with her self-criticism. When he did not do so, she began to recall something of the origins of the particular belief.[11]

That the conditions of safety or happy endings have been satisfied, that the therapist has passed the test, would become evident in a young person's willingness to enter into increasingly threatening tensions and necessary contradictions of life and development. The safety of the ending provides hope and joy enough to enable the emergence of previously suppressed pain. Pain now finally may be suffered instead of apathetically or aggressively resisted, repressed, or denied. Notice that the young person cannot *create* the promise or the happy ending but instead only *receives* it, in turn entering into the increasing tension it inaugurates. The counselee cannot bring about the counselor's response to the given test, nor his or her own healing.

What one begins to hear on the distant horizon of these therapeutic happy endings are resonant tones of eschatological hope, which anticipate the possibility of a gradually opening or suddenly received future. Such hope is not wishful thinking, nor escapist or utopian, but rather, as Paul Pruyser puts it in the epigraph of this chapter, humanly grounded in "the experience of doubting, fearing and despairing," hope "steering a ship in a gale."

This tenuous hope emerges as a result of the counselor's making and keeping certain promises. The counselor implicitly promises, for example, to carefully confront destructive behaviors or beliefs, to avoid being manipulated or seduced by the young person, and to match or mirror in timely fashion the adolescent's newly emerging interests or transformations of narcissism. Hope emerges for the youth and caregiver alike from the fulfillment of these implied therapeutic contracts. Passing such tests of safety and keeping such promises are relatively easy to talk about in theoretical abstraction, of course, but more difficult to discern and administer in the crucible of therapeutic work. Troubled young people, after all, can pose an almost limitless range of potential tests of safety to those who would assist them, but from this intense and intricate relational dance is fashioned embryonic hope.

Hope as Safety
for Ultimate Negations

The work of the psychological theorists here, as well as the case studies of John Turner and Stan, indicate that internal strivings for wholeness in troubled youth consistently have been thwarted by broken promises and unhappy endings, significantly compromising the safety and hope necessary for entering even relatively benign forms of realistic suffering. Instead of being able to sustain necessary suffering, we notice Stan and John Turner attempting to self-contain their loss and pain, cut off from future hope and present intimacy in every human relationship. Theories of therapy and transformation, secular or pastoral, become then essential guides to the difficult and intricate administration of conditions of safety, given the unique and peculiar tests posed by each particular young person.

May we not argue further that *all* persons, at any point along a spectrum of mental health or illness, face certain tensions, contradictions, or conflicts so overwhelming or unfathomable to the life of the self that no human being could guarantee the longed-for conditions of safety? What promising parent, therapist, pastor, institution, corporation, or community could pass the tests of safety or assure the happy ending for situations involving the senseless suffering of little children or adolescent victims of incest, for the massive holocausts of this century or the destruction of nature, for the silencing of entire populations and special classifications of persons, or even any individual's own death? These and other ultimate threats annihilate the foundations of safety and hope for even the strongest of selves, begging happy endings of justice, mercy, and redemption that no promising individual or agency could possibly apportion. In order to enter into the tension posed by these supreme perils, would we not need the assurance of a happy ending beyond even their extreme power of negation, even death itself?

It is this definitive promise of safety, involving the supreme suffering of abandonment, that is at the heart of the eschatological claims of Jesus Christ and the Christian life of faith. Such an ending could only be received, not humanly created. If realized, it would enable persons, individually and collectively, to enter ever more extreme experiences of negation and death, not in escapist flights of fancy or willful self-destruction, but in compellingly satisfying attitudes of joyful sadness and suffering hope.

Here, the nature of the particular future, the particular ending one experiences in the present, and the *ultimacy* of that future or ending, have as significant an impact on the life of the self as the nature of one's past experiences. Indeed, the nature of one's future experience actually *creates* one's past and present experiences. Such a claim initially seems an odd departure from developmental theory, but we are proposing instead that developmental and eschatological theories are vitally complementary companions. Each seeks to open proximate or ultimate horizons of redemptive hope through enlarging repertoires of necessary suffering for those caught in tyrannical throes of abandonment and despair.

Diligent Perseverance and Joyful Interruption

How then are the selves of developmental psychology and eschatological theology fundamentally related? Does the notion of an eschatological self, the awaited self yet to be revealed, usurp in any way the familiar self of developmental psychology, the self we seem to carry with us through the ordinary days and times of our lives?

Eschatological theology claims that time moves not in one but two directions. It moves in the familiar course of chronological time, from past to future, that is witnessed in the rhythms of nature and human development through the life cycle, is vital for prediction and planning, and is experienced in our sense of becoming. But time also treks a less familiar eschatological path, from future to past or, better, from eternity into history, a path necessary for discerning meaning in history and a path for hope of transformation and surprising new possibilities, one experienced as coming toward us from outside ourselves, as startling breakthrough.

This sense of coming to oneself in eschatological time, however astonishing in each individual instance, is nonetheless a familiar component of any intensive process of creative discernment or discovery, including scientific innovation, although it is not always given due consideration. In every successful process of counseling, pastoral or otherwise, for example, there are times that can best be described as moments of joyful interruption, surprising to both counselor and counseled alike, that contribute in large measure to the healing process. These startling intrusions are experienced as coming from beyond the self, from out of the blue, we say, or "It just struck me . . . ," or "You won't believe what just happened . . . ." Such moments have the effect of instilling hope in, as well as blurring distinctions between, both giver and receiver of care. In those circumstances where such interruptions come to hold more than a fleeting significance, generating instead an enduring reconstitution of the self-in-relation, caregiver and young person together play witness to the advent of God's new creation.[12] For the counselor to fail to notice the uniqueness of such moments or make no attempt to understand their full mystery would be to perform a great disservice to those whom we seek to assist.

Developmental theory necessarily seeks to show the importance of how best to assist the youth in our care in becoming new persons. Eschatological theology additionally challenges us to expect the coming of something new, a type of healing beyond therapeutic prediction and control. Developmental psychology requires of the counselor a rigorous, analytical way of knowing the young person in the intricate details of his or her unique contexts and historical circumstances of trauma and need. Eschatological theology demands of the counselor a "knowing" in the sense of experiencing with mysterious wonder the whole of the young person as one caught up along with the counselor alike by the Spirit of the living God into the passionate and triumphant new creation of Jesus Christ. In the therapeutic context the eschatological event, like the disciples' experience of Jesus risen from the dead, involves a surprising reversal of previously destructive patterns, experienced by counselor and young person not as their own achievement but as a gift that elicits joyful awe, in turn providing the safety necessary for experiencing more realistic suffering for the sake of right relationships. A deep complementarity thus begins to surface between developmental and eschatological trajectories of self experience.

Eschatological hope likely can be distinguished from expectations for change present in clinical psychologies by eschatology's concentration on ultimate matters, that is, hope beyond the negation of death. Allowing entrance of eschatological awareness into developmental therapies may nudge them beyond the vital preliminary task of reopening the young person to the possibility of any future at all, by raising the question of which particular future and the ultimacy of that future the counselor is attempting to open. Any therapist, after all, is at least implicitly holding up a more or less adequate image of *some* future.

The developmental clinician must press the pastoral counselor to be grounded in the intricate and tireless work of detailed contextual analysis, informed psychological acuity, and accountability for understanding the unique life circumstances of the young person. The eschatological counselor, in turn, must press the psychologist to expect the unexpected in the healing process, to discern the whole of the adolescent as greater than the sum of the parts, and to examine as honestly as possible the ultimacy of the future hope that the counselor purveys.

Christian theology's bold claim is that one particular future promises therapeutic safety for sustaining hope in the midst of even severe negations to life of evil and injustice, and natural disaster and death—namely, the future of Jesus Christ. The foundation for this claim is the tension inherent in the cross and resurrection of Christ. The cross demands that ultimate hope must never be identified with wishful thinking or escapist behavior but instead be grounded in the suffering and shame of embodied human life. The resurrection, on the other hand, insists that even the ultimate "reality principle" of realistic suffering, evil, and death will be superseded by a finally more real "pleasure principle" beyond all earthly imagining, and that no abandonment in life or death will be able to separate God from God's creation.

Resurrection without the cross, hope without suffering, pleasure without reality, heavenly glory without earthly history, and eschatological possibility without developmental necessity all lead to escapism and the degradation of the human body and the natural earth. Likewise, cross without resurrection, suffering without hope, reality without pleasure, history without eternity, and developmental necessity without eschatological possibility lead to devastating apathy and despair. This dialectic, promised in history in the person of Jesus Christ, is the heart of an eschatological therapy, offering conditions of safety necessary for entering with joyful sadness even into death itself.

An Eschatological Reprise of Stan

Returning to Stan's work in therapy, we see evidence for both a blocked future and an emerging hope. We previously discussed signs of Stan's lost future, including significant expressions of childhood anxiety, premonitions of disasters and early death, and panic attacks by night. But there is also indication of an activation of both *futurum* (a sense of becoming a self) and *adventus* (a sense of coming to himself) in Stan's process of therapy.

We notice the former in Stan's growing trust in the therapeutic process and relationship, perhaps most clearly surfacing at times when my own therapeutic inadequacies threatened that trust, as when I tried to press Stan into attending Narcotics Anonymous against his will. Once these failures of empathy or broken therapeutic promises were recognized, usually through the input of my supervisor, some semblance of safety was restored, leading to more honest conversation from both sides concerning frustrations in our relationship. Stan, in turn, connected these present events in therapy to similar experiences in past relationships, contributing to a growing sense of continuity for him, a developing *futurum* hope that such patterns could be recognized and overcome.

None of this, however, prepared Stan for the sudden inbreaking of *adventus*, perhaps most evident in his self-transcending spiritual experience. Strikingly, Stan described this event much like he previously spoke of his panic attacks—as an intense, physical sensation beyond his control moving up through his body. But unlike earlier attacks, this experience did not "scramble his brain." Quite to the contrary, it soothed and calmed him— as if it were a "peace attack"—with power compelling enough to negate previous contradictions and fragmentation. The incident seemed literally to propel Stan into experiences of intra- and interpersonal harmony. While Stan had no traditional religious language by which to name it, he nonetheless recognized its transformative power, often recounting the event as hope inspiring even months after the fact. Both Stan and I experienced this intrusion as one brought about by neither of us but as one that contributed significantly to our work together.

This breakthrough is best described not as one perpetuating Stan's previous patterns and expectations, nor a mere continuation of Stan's ordinary progress in therapy, but as an interruption that had the effect of infusing new hope. That this inbreaking of feeling was different from any of Stan's previous drug trips, in which we might presume he felt similar sensations or saw comparable bright lights, is recognized most clearly in its reality factor, leading to necessary suffering or joyful sadness and transforming, however momentarily, Stan's relationships with self and others. It launched him into his first honest conversation with Jennifer, into joyful reconciliation in another deeply disaffected friendship with the boy who overdosed, and even into previously uncharted depths of sadness in Stan's childhood.

This is not to suggest that this eschatological peak experience served as some final resting place in our work together. To the contrary, in my desire to help Stan acknowledge and explore his *adventus* experience, I failed to brace for the rush of previous defenses or to steer toward a necessary return to the more tedious labors of *futurum*, which led to an interruption in his therapy. Yet the singular power of Stan's eschatological moment should not be dismissed. Like the early disciples' experience of Jesus' resurrection, Stan's mysterious experience of congruence involved a shattering reversal of previously entrenched patterns, was felt to be not an achievement but a gift that elicited joy, and provided safety enough for him to enter into more realistic suffering for the sake of right relationships.

It may be presumptuous to suggest that, in his experience of *adventus*, Stan was experiencing the Spirit or presence of Jesus Christ, since Stan himself possessed no language for or awareness of any such holy visitation. May we not more modestly submit, however, that the claims of eschatological theology need not conflict with basic tenets of developmental psychology, both understandings fundamentally affirming that future hope is opened through appropriate relationships of commitment and love in all their painful complexities? Stan's eschatological self surprises his developing self with a promise of the self Stan one day may cherish—congruent, integrated, peaceful, and capable of suffering rather than defending against the pain of broken relationships and ubiquitous death. While unwilling to name this experience using traditional religious language, Stan recognized it as promoting, not contradicting, the mission of his developing self, a calling highly congruent with the proclaimed future of Christ.

This discussion of Stan should not tempt us to conclude that the eschatological self consists solely in peak experiences of self-transcending illumination. Moments of *adventus* are but one movement of the eschatological self, only one of its vectors, the other of which navigates the stormy seas and earthly tedium of *futurum*. A prominent chemist once said to me, "The solution always comes as a surprise to those who discipline themselves for the search." This statement suggests perhaps another way to express the eschatological self's moving to rhythms of both discipline and surprise, of search and surrender, of soulful depths and spiritual heights, of becoming and coming.

John Turner and the Eschatological Self

Near the end of Elijah Anderson's account of his informal mentoring relationship with John Turner, the youth emerges as a drug dealer on a street corner in Baltimore, shot in the gut and carrying around a "bag" for the rest of his life, less than a model of triumph for the eschatological self. We are left to ask what went wrong, what could have been different, if anything at all, while we are also given to ponder the tenacity of hope even there, amid John's tragic social and emotional theater. If in John Turner's story we have difficulty discerning more dramatic expressions of the eschatological self, we yet may glimpse its more modest influences.

From the outset of the relationship between Turner and Anderson, various factors congealed in leading John to implore the assistance of a complete stranger. We may interpret John's plea for help as an initial unconscious test of the degree of safety Anderson could provide, a precondition for hope. Clearly Anderson succeeded in passing this and others of John's early tests. He made and kept promises to find a lawyer for John and to be present at his court hearing, where the judge's leniency relieved all concerned. Recall John later saying he thanked God that Anderson had come into his life to help him, then adding, "I didn't think people did that anymore." Through quite concrete initiatives on John's behalf, coupled with an empathic engaging of his hungry soul, Anderson began cultivating a safe space in which to sow for John seeds of hope.

A similar pattern became evident some months later, when Anderson helped John acquire a more lucrative hospital job under Curtis Hardy's tutelage. John expressed to Anderson his discouraging job prospects; Anderson spoke to Hardy, and John grew enthusiastic about his expanding future horizons. In this sequence John tested the pathogenic belief that he was worthless and unemployable; Anderson disconfirmed the belief by securing for John a solid job, thus passing the test; and this in turn led John to joyful release and enhanced hope, propelling him into increasing complexities of adult life. One sees the eschatological self here as a necessarily relational web, a mutually engaging self, at once actively initiating or persistently "becoming," yet also passively received or graciously "coming" from another.

Within these hope-engendering dramas of courtroom and workplace lurked more ominous threats to John's self as well, his eschatological hope no elegant drifting in a Venetian gondola, to borrow Pruyser's image. At the court hearing, for example, Anderson noticed how John's probation officer turned cold to him when he mentioned his association with John. And in their meeting concerning the hospital job, Anderson perceived Curtis Hardy's reluctance to vouch for someone he believed to be at great risk.

Anderson sensed that he could not sustain John's precarious self single-handedly, in part because the protective resin of John's street persona had already begun to set, likely firmly, by the time of their initial contact. When Anderson repeatedly attempted to widen John's circle of support, he soon discovered subtle but formidable barriers: the owner of the Italian restaurant appreciated John's diligent work but paid him poorly and erratically, while tolerating racial slurs directed at John by white workers; the lawyers Anderson found to represent John carried out their tasks decently, if reluctantly at times, but then exited; the hospital coworkers took John under their care but then, through tactics perceived by John as shaming, pressured him to change; the probation officers, themselves only precariously removed from John's own station in life, failed to balance appropriate discipline with encouraging support, resulting in confused role and generational boundaries; and even the Army recruiter and the government he represented would have nothing to do with a young man on probation. Whatever their individual motivations and quandaries, collectively they represented for John a landscape littered with broken promises and hostile to the gestation of safety and hope. Anderson alone seemed humanly poised as midwife for John's eschatological self.

Drained by John's voracious appetite for unrequited empathy, however, Anderson drew on gradually diminishing rations of hope on John's behalf, a victim of his own empathic success. From the perspective of the present schema, Anderson eventually felt compelled to deliberately fail John's escalating tests for therapeutic safety, culminating in Anderson's offering John the $150 he requested and thereby intentionally severing their ties.

Even at so decisive a juncture as this, is all hope extinguished for John? On their last day together Anderson sensed a deepening intimacy with John, paradoxically evident in John's derisive accusation that Anderson was "naive" for failing to have more influence with the Army recruiter and later, after Anderson helped him get another restaurant job, in John's revealing how he had felt used by the woman who refused him visitation of his sons. Anderson rightly considered this glimmer of relational honesty—what theologically may be recognized as the perseverance of John's eschatological self—"really a major development in [their] relationship."[13]

If so unremarkable a breakthrough depicts the genesis of hope in the depleted self of a troubled youth—a younger and an older man conversationally sparring in a Philadelphia restaurant—then it becomes clear how readily the workings of the eschatological self could be slighted amid more dramatic youthful vicissitudes of violence or depression. But hope is fertilized in such ordinary soil as this. The eschatological self undeniably works its wonders of decisive transformation in the surprising rush of *adventus*, but typically only in tandem with the more modest, discerning labors of *futurum*. Hope comes as a surprise to those who discipline themselves for the search.

Chapter Seven

The Case of Laurie

I like to hurt myself, because it makes me feel better.
—Laurie, to her therapist[1]

This and the following chapter explore the contours of the eschatological self by focusing on two additional case studies of troubled young people. As they unfold, the stories of "Laurie" and of Bobby Griffith will sound starkly familiar, since both youths share characteristics of the so-called borderline and narcissistic self disorders. Their struggles serve in part to reinforce what has been said already concerning Stan and John Turner. Yet unique dilemmas surface as well in the present cases, particularly concerning politically and theologically volatile issues surrounding gender expectations, sexual violence, and sexual orientation. Each case suggests intractable links between the eschatological self and politics, faith, and culture, and speaks as well to the disturbing possibility that, in their efforts to heal, caregivers inadvertently may maim, even kill, the impressionable adolescent self.

"I Like to Hurt Myself, Because It Makes Me Feel Better"

In late April, several weeks before her sixteenth birthday, Laurie was admitted to an inpatient adolescent treatment facility in a small Midwestern city by her state's Department of Human Services. This was only the most recent of a string of hospitalizations, institutionalizations, and foster placements that had marked Laurie's life over the previous several years. Her prospects for remaining at this new center for any length of time were grim, since she had a long history of running away from whatever family or facility in which she was placed, including, and perhaps especially, the homes of her biological parents.

Laurie was assigned to her room in the attractive group home that housed in separate wings approximately twelve other male and female adolescents who, like her, were diagnosed with multiple problems involving substance abuse, depression, and additional evidence of "acting out" or "conduct disorder." She was met at the center by staff therapist Dr. Sarah Rand, a soft-spoken mainline Protestant minister in her mid-thirties who, beyond her seminary training, held an advanced degree specializing in feminist approaches to marriage and family therapy. What follows is my composite rendering of the case drawn from the case notes of and several interviews with Dr. Rand, as well as one ninety-minute interview near the time of her discharge that I myself was allowed with Laurie in the presence of her therapist.

Laurie was a pleasant, working-class, white youth of medium height and build, with brownish-blonde hair and fair skin and of average intelligence. She had a nominal Roman Catholic background, yet never thought of herself as religious in belief or practice. She considered, however, her deceased maternal grandfather as her beneficent "higher power" and held an image of God that resembled the portrait of a gentle, kindly Jesus that once hung in her maternal grandparents' home.

In an early admissions interview, Laurie indicated that, in addition to her history of substance abuse, she was depressed, was having trouble falling asleep, and was experiencing increased appetite with related concerns of gaining weight, all complicated by past episodes of bulimic binges and purging. She said, "I am always suicidal," and showed scars from carvings she had attempted on her arms and legs. But later in the same initial interview she contradicted herself, saying that she had never been suicidal. She also confessed to sometimes pulling her hair, explaining, "I like to hurt myself, because it makes me feel better." Laurie had an extensive history of drug abuse; she had used crack cocaine, speed, and LSD, had sniffed nail polish remover, and for some years had abused alcohol, drinking at times to the point of losing consciousness. She previously had been arrested for public intoxication and falsifying information to the police, and admitted as well to stealing, running away from home, spray-painting cars, and truancy. She had been on probation for a number of years.

Laurie also readily announced, "I have been having sex since four days before my twelfth birthday," and reported a history of sexual abuse from around age five by her babysitter's boyfriend and many times since by, among others, the boyfriend of her best friend's mother at age eleven and by one or two of her mother's boyfriends and ex-husbands, although never by her biological father. She had had sexual relations with more than thirteen perpetrators of abuse and some purportedly consensual sexual partners since age twelve and likewise hinted that she may have been raped by a boy on a recent "run" from a previous institution. She at times had worked as a prostitute. She now had at least one sexually transmitted disease and wondered too if she might be pregnant. Laurie was admitted to the adolescent group home with a tentative diagnosis of borderline personality disorder with substance abuse, and her prognosis was guarded.

In her first meeting with Laurie, Dr. Rand learned that she had recently run from another adolescent treatment facility in a neighboring city. She was now being placed here by her father, Carl, who had asked the Department of Human Services for assistance in the face of his own increasing helplessness in caring for her. In her early therapy sessions, including this one, tears often welled up in Laurie's eyes; she was especially concerned about whether she would be accepted by her peers in this new program. She also said that she had a fiancé and would be married soon, although she never mentioned this man nor any engagement or marriage plans again. Laurie had completed her sophomore year of high school and had recently lived at and run away from the home of her father and stepmother, Helen, in another city. She somewhat proudly mentioned that, including foster placements, she had moved twenty-six times in her life.

Laurie had no memories of her biological parents ever having lived together, nor, she confessed, could she even imagine such a possibility because "they're total opposites." Carl and Kathy divorced when Laurie was an infant and her only biological brother, Ben, two years older, was just a toddler. Both parents had since remarried, her mother five times and her father once. Laurie reported that her earliest childhood memories involved images that included her parents' new spouses. She remembered as a two-year-old anxiously clinging to her father's leg as Laurie met her stepmother, Helen, for the first time. She recalled as a three-year-old riding around in the orange sports car of her mother's third husband, as together they went grocery shopping shortly after the wedding. At the time of Laurie's admission, Carl remained married to Helen, and Kathy had been married to her husband, Michael, for the past five years.

Laurie lived almost exclusively with her mother and her mother's husbands until she was thirteen years old. Then, after a brief stay at her maternal grandmother's home, she moved in with her father and stepmother. Carl visited Laurie and Ben every second weekend throughout their childhood. Carl, age forty, had graduated from high school and now enjoyed economic stability as a union assembly-line worker; Kathy, now thirty-seven, did not finish high school and, with two dependent children, only recently gained a financial foothold, even that still tentative from Laurie's perspective. Laurie remembered growing up on welfare, using food stamps and relying on Goodwill for clothing. Once, in the second grade, she tattled on another classmate, for which Laurie received a spanking from her teacher in front of the class. When her mother heard of this, Kathy marched to the school "drunk or high," in Laurie's words, in order to "beat up" the teacher.

Laurie moved from place to place in those early years, but at times lived in a trailer home near her maternal grandparents. She fondly remembered her frequent treks with Ben to their grandparents' home, where she felt secure and loved and "never got in trouble." Her grandparents also had another child, Kathy's sister Kelly, just six months older than Laurie. Aunt and niece, in a relationship more akin to cousins, enjoyed a rich friendship. The three children liked to play with dolls, Kelly and Ben with his G. I. Joes and Laurie with one of her many beloved Barbies, whom she delighted in dressing in their "beautiful clothes," because with Barbie, Laurie said, "I got to be in control of somebody."

"Nothing She Does Surprises Me Anymore"

Of Laurie's parents and stepparents, only Carl appeared willing to meet in therapy sessions, and he at some sacrifice since he lived nearly 100 miles from the group home. Dr. Rand sensed that Carl seemed genuinely concerned for his daughter's well-being and was willing to cooperate in her care. He wanted to work toward bringing Laurie back to his home but also lamented that possibility, given the likelihood of her eventually running away. "Nothing she does surprises me anymore," Carl told Rand, who perceived him as both supportive of and angry with Laurie, as well as helpless in the face of her frequent flights.

Carl also told Rand that Helen, who had four grown children of her own from a previous marriage, had felt "burned" by family therapy sessions at another institution and now refused to participate in them. Rand nonetheless attempted to invite Helen to therapy, believing her an important link in preparing for Laurie's return to their home; but, as Carl predicted, Helen declined. Carl would later privately tell Rand that he dreaded one day having to choose between living with his daughter or his wife, since he loved them both deeply. He expressed disdain for Laurie's biological mother Kathy and her husband, whom Carl believed were alcoholics and smoked marijuana, although he thought that Michael recently had been through a drug treatment program and that Kathy had claimed to stop drinking.

Carl agreed to join his daughter in counseling sessions with Dr. Rand once every other week. Rand additionally would see Laurie at least twice each week at the group home, with some informal or drop-in visits. Rand was encouraged by Carl's willingness to participate but wrote in her case notes that "writing a new history" for this family would likely involve a great deal of creative energy. For her part, Laurie seemed glad to be at this new facility and settled into working the twelve-step program based on Alcoholics Anonymous required of her there.

A Rape on a Run

Two weeks after arriving, Laurie wanted to speak with Rand about a possible rape experience while on a run from a previous institution. Laurie was not clear concerning differences between rape and sexual exploration, since something akin to rape was sexually normative for her. She initially doubted her ability to distinguish abuse from intimacy. Rand sought to assist her in differentiating them by asking, "What kind of man do you want?" or "What's a 'real' man to you?" or "How do you want to be treated?" Significantly, Rand also requested Laurie's permission to follow through with rape crisis intervention, including pursuing the possibility of a criminal investigation. Laurie readily agreed to both requests and, much later in their relationship, confessed that Dr. Rand was the first person to take seriously her reports of rape, which set her apart from previous therapists.

Yet all was not smooth sailing between client and therapist. Just one week later Laurie was annoyed with Rand for wanting to discuss the criminal investigation of the rape in the presence of her father. Earlier, Laurie had phoned to inform her stepmother of the rape and the investigation that Rand instigated on her behalf. Now in the joint session with Carl, Laurie refused her father's attempts to provide comfort or assistance, although they sat huddled closely together on the same sofa. Rand began to notice in this meeting Laurie's tendency to take peculiar delight in sharing with her father, indeed with anyone who would listen, explicit details of this rape or her sexual experiences. Rand sought to guide Laurie instead to delimit her conversation with her father to the fact of the rape and the details of the investigation. But this demarcation of boundaries concerning sexual conversation provoked Laurie's wrath.

Her father, by contrast, was relieved by this intervention, acknowledging his discomfort at Laurie's descriptions of her many sexual encounters. Laurie, now more depressed, began to talk more reflectively about ambivalence concerning her sexuality, promiscuity, and quest for sobriety. At one moment she said that she never wanted to be a parent; at the next, that she was trying to become pregnant.

Carl, too, was irritable and ambivalent in this session, demanding that Rand not allow Laurie to interrupt his wife at work by phoning with details concerning her treatment. Yet he was more hopeful now than before that Helen would be willing to participate in family therapy sessions as

Laurie's discharge date neared. He also gave Rand and Laurie permission to phone Laurie's biological mother if the need arose.

Brightening Prospects

The following weeks provided guarded hope that things were gradually beginning to turn around. Laurie happily celebrated her sixteenth birthday with her father, slowly advanced in her twelve-step program goals, became less demanding on the group home staff, and grew in her assertiveness and communication skills with peers in her unit. In the past, for example, if Laurie received food or treats from her father during his visits, she would feel obligated to relinquish them to the male residents to avoid alienating them. Rand noticed this pattern and pointed out that Laurie's peers would not likely reciprocate her generosity by sharing their treats with her, so neither did she need to indulge their demands of her. This was another in a series of boundary-setting lessons that helped Laurie begin to differentiate mutuality from exploitation, and she seemed receptive to such instruction.

As her therapist continued to confront these and other, especially sexual, boundary issues, Laurie's depression increasingly surfaced. She shared with Rand feelings of degradation for having a sexually transmitted disease and expressed her realization that when painful feelings surfaced, she wanted to hurt herself physically, so as to anesthetize herself. Getting high, having sex, and experiencing hangovers all distracted her from emotional pain. Laurie also had begun to write down and appropriately share with her father both her resentments of and apologies to him, one component of her twelve-step program.

Rand also wondered aloud with Carl and Laurie concerning Laurie's frequent medical complaints and desire to go to a doctor for any minor ache or pain. In her first months of treatment, Laurie requested medical help daily. Once, for instance, Laurie was certain that she had lost a filling in a tooth, but a dentist confirmed that all fillings were accounted for. Carl speculated that her mother's extensive family history of cancer—Laurie's maternal grandfather died of cancer several years prior; her mother suffered and survived two bouts of lung cancer and Hodgkin's disease, and her aunt Kelly, Laurie's age, already had lost her leg to cancer—may have contributed to Laurie's anxieties concerning her health. Carl was tiring, however, of Laurie's many medical bills and said he would welcome any relief from her frequent visits to physicians. Laurie was upset by her father's complaints, and Rand attempted to intervene by helping Laurie begin to differentiate between a desire for attention and a need for medical care: "If you need attention, Laurie, it's OK just to tell someone that you need attention. We all need attention sometimes. It doesn't have to come from the doctor."

Open conversations such as these inspired hope in Laurie, Carl, and Dr. Rand, and now, two months into Laurie's treatment, everyone seemed cautiously optimistic about the possibility of Laurie's eventual homecoming. Rand privately worried, however, about Helen's absence and its potential to quickly unravel these initial gains. She also regretted not having attempted to involve Laurie's mother, Kathy, and stepfather, Michael, from the outset. In addition, Rand noticed Laurie's ongoing boundary problems with the boys on her unit. She would sit too closely to the boys during group discussions and, until a staff member intervened to retrieve it, recently had given one boy her ring to wear. Rand likewise worried about the intensity of Laurie's surfacing depression and requested a psychiatric consultation to determine whether antidepressant medication might be helpful, to which the psychiatrist agreed.

"I Like to Have Sex When I Get Bored"

By early July, Rand was seeing extensive mood swings in Laurie during their joint sessions with Carl. Her affect would range from happy to tearful to resentful to accepting within a single meeting. Laurie returned from a successful day-pass home visit with Carl and Helen, but Carl reported that Laurie continued to want to discuss all the "gory details" of her personal life, this time concerning the painful medical treatment for her sexually transmitted disease. Laurie was tearful, upset about her father's not wanting to hear about her sexual life. Rand again reminded Laurie of what was and was not appropriate for her to share with her father in this regard, noting that her father was neither her counselor nor buddy, but her parent. Carl was willing to hear and continue to support Laurie's speaking about general information concerning her medical treatment and sexuality, but not about explicit sexual actions or "sex gossip." They all agreed that if Laurie needed to talk about sexual issues in the future, she could call her mother but was not to use her father as sexual confidant. This resolution appeared acceptable to everyone involved, and Laurie seemed glad to have been able to talk with Carl honestly and openly.

Later that evening, after what seemed to Rand this productive session, a staff member discovered in a boy's room five letters that Laurie had written revealing sexual experiences with him and other boys since entering the program. She wrote, "I'm going to have sex with you like you've never had it before . . . ," and "Let's get together and do it . . . ." Rand confronted Laurie late that evening, who told of kissing one boy on an excursion to the public library, giving another boy a "hand job"—stimulating him at a movie theater during another recreational outing—and of her being touched or "finger-banged" by boys at the swimming pool and while play-ing cards in the group home. Although Laurie confessed to instigating some of these actions herself, because "I like to have sex when I get bored," at least one of the boys had coerced her into sexual favors by discovering and threatening to expose her contraband cigarettes. When Rand learned of this, the boy was disciplined and legal charges filed against him, although he remained on the unit. Laurie clearly was upset at having to talk about these things with her therapist, although Rand assured her that Laurie's own well-being was most essential to her.

Laurie remained uncomfortable the next morning, not wanting to see or eat with her male peers. Indeed, she was prevented by the staff from any further proximity to the three boys involved, an intervention Laurie wel-comed. Rand assured her that the prohibitions were protective, not puni-tive, although she also expressed disappointment that Laurie had not requested staff intercession regarding the coercion of sexual favors.

Rand called Carl around noon, relaying information concerning the re-cent chain of events. Carl said he realized that sexual issues went to the heart of his daughter's problems. Rand, too, had become convinced that Laurie's sexual addiction and promiscuity were primary problems, al-though linked to her substance abuse as well.

Within weeks, however, now three months into her treatment, the cri-sis mood had passed, and DHS officials visited the center to formulate dis-charge plans for Laurie. Everyone again expressed a desire that Helen be involved with the discharge process and with Laurie's ongoing health is-sues. Laurie wanted to return home before the beginning of the new school year. Carl hoped that she could be granted a forty-eight-hour home-visit pass within the coming month, and Rand reminded them of the twelve-step program goals Laurie would need to meet prior to receiving those privileges. Therapy continued to focus on respect and boundary issues, un-til the time came for Rand's two-week summer vacation.

"I Don't Want to Live with You, Dad"

When Rand returned near the beginning of August, Laurie seemed fur-ther than ever from graduating from her program or nearing discharge. Two minutes into their joint session, Laurie blurted out to her father, "I don't want to live with you, Dad. I can't get a clean start in that town." While Rand was on vacation, Laurie had enjoyed a wonderful visit to her father's home. Rand learned only later that, while at home, Laurie confided in a friend concerning her sexually transmitted disease, and the girl in turn spread the word around town. Exasperated and helpless in the face of Lau-rie's sudden belligerence about returning home, Carl expressed that this was the "old Laurie" coming out again. Rand excused Laurie, then instructed Carl to find out what had changed her mind.

Discharge plans continued, but Rand decided to meet with Laurie individually as soon as possible, as well as to order a review of Laurie's medications. Laurie continued to express her sense that she was not yet ready to return home. They also discussed the ongoing police investigations of her rape.

Shortly thereafter, Laurie ran away from the group home. However familiar the pattern in Laurie's own life, her run was devastating for Sarah Rand, who cried in a session with her own supervisor, wondering what her months of work with Laurie had meant. Her supervisor comforted Rand, saying only, "You got close to her." When Laurie returned five days later, she repeated to Rand a tale not unlike those of previous runs from other institutions—a story of prostitution, another rape, and living in intoxicated squalor. She was sheepish and tearful. She told Rand, "It feels like you've given up on me," to which Rand replied, "No, I haven't given up, although I am angry and I don't want to hear any more right now about your escapades." Laurie said that she had "hit bottom" and wanted to change. Rand remained unconvinced and proceeded to order pregnancy, HIV, and other medical tests.

Laurie's run sealed within Carl a decision to prevent her from returning to live with him. He tried to share openly with his daughter the emotions he felt while she was on the run, but Laurie was too overwhelmed with her own guilt and grief to hear him. He released custody to Kathy, trying to convince himself that Laurie's mother had the potential to provide her an acceptable home. Rand was clearly concerned for Carl's change of heart, for she had never met Kathy nor had any significant contact to determine whether her home would be an acceptable placement. In a phone conversation, Kathy indicated to Rand that she was willing to have Laurie live with her but unwilling to participate in any family therapy sessions. So Rand arranged instead for a conference call where Laurie, Kathy, and Rand could talk about the many unresolved issues.

Discharge planning continued for several weeks. Dr. Rand contacted DHS concerning the need for a visit to Kathy's home in order to determine its suitability and kept meeting with Laurie individually. She had additional lengthy phone conversations with Kathy, who was following through with various "homework" assignments that Rand had given her. Rand sought out information from Kathy regarding past sexual abuse perpetrators and Laurie's history of victimization. Still, given Kathy's reluctance to participate in family sessions, and few indications of progress during Laurie's residential treatment, Rand remained unconvinced that Laurie should be released any time soon.

"I Want What I Want When I Want It"

As it turned out, the decision concerning discharge was removed from Sarah Rand's own hand. A week or so later, Laurie eagerly met Rand as she arrived for her shift on the unit and queried, "Sarah, what do you think of my discharge?" Caught off guard, Rand replied, "What discharge?" Laurie informed Rand that DHS had ordered her discharge within the next two weeks, without inquiring of or informing Laurie's therapist herself. Rand kept her feelings in check in Laurie's presence, but later acknowledged to me her frustration and anger that a discharge was ordered by state officials prior to Laurie's graduation from the final levels of her treatment program and without any consultation with Rand. She wondered of Laurie, "Will she make it to eighteen? Will she ever have a stable, healthy life?"

Resigned to the realities of state-funded programs, Rand scheduled a discharge meeting. Laurie, Carl, Kathy, Michael, and Laurie's childhood playmate/aunt Kelly all came. They talked, among other things, of Laurie's relationship with Sarah. Laurie spoke of how she initially hated Rand but of how recently she had told a new girl on the unit that "Sarah is really OK, once you get to know her." Carl said to Rand, "Won't you be glad to get rid of her?", to which she responded, "No, I really like Laurie and have enjoyed working with your daughter." At this, Kathy's eyes watered as she said, "In all our work with therapists, no one has ever said anything positive about her."

In an interview that I myself conducted with Laurie only a few days later, just prior to her leaving the group home, she sat comfortably curled on Rand's office sofa, wearing a stylish "No Fear" sweatshirt. I asked Laurie as she reflected back whether any one thought, belief, or philosophy guided her through life. At first, she responded by saying, "I wish I would've listened to my parents. That's the advice I'd give a ten-year-old girl—⁶Listen to your parents. They know what they're talking about. When they say "No," they *mean* "No," and that's that.'" Only moments later, however, as she continued to ponder my question, her second thought initially seemed to contradict the first. "I guess," she said, "my philosophy is that no one's going to tell me what to do. I want what I want when I want it. That's the way it is with me." But perhaps in Laurie's mind the two lessons were not as irreconcilable as they first appeared. For when I asked who taught her to want what she wants when she wants it, she immediately responded with undisguised delight, "My parents!"

I likewise asked her to look forward, although it quickly became evident that her future vision was clouded—she could vaguely imagine perhaps a minimum-wage job or something. She could name no adult she particularly admired or aspired to emulate. Instead, she would live simply "one day at a time, one step at a time," she said, citing the Alcoholics Anonymous credo. Then suddenly she remembered a quote from her beloved maternal grandfather, himself an alcoholic who now in death served as her higher power: "If you have one foot in yesterday and one foot in tomorrow, you're pissing all over today."

Witnessing to Hope

Laurie's case, like those of John Turner and Stan, has less than a storybook ending, tempting caregivers to despair of penetrating her shield of apathy and self-destruction. But precisely for their severity, Laurie's circumstances provide suitably challenging terrain on which to consider claims for the eschatological self.

Recall that the eschatological self is a way of expressing the conviction, based on the shocking reversal of death in the resurrection of Jesus, that no person fully possesses his or her own self. One's self in large part remains held in trust, penultimately by others, ultimately by God in Christ, and is glimpsed or revealed at only infrequent moments of great clarity or confusion, of ecstasy or shame, instances of coming to one's self or senses. These essential *adventus* experiences, while likely much less rare than we are accustomed to believe, are but one generative movement of the eschatological self. Authentic hope—or, at least, its receptive soil—accumulates developmentally as well, through often arcane, imperfect human transactions involving promises made and kept, or broken and confessed, in the more ordinary rhythms of *futurum*.

Even as eschatological hope in Christian theology arose from the ashes of the cross, so too does the pastoral caregiver anticipate emergence of Laurie's eschatological self, not apart from the hopeless circumstances of her life but out of their very midst. The burden of the eschatological clinician becomes then one of clinging unceasingly to hope, with caregiver as resolute sleuth of hope, tracking even less-than-promising leads that might suggest the divine presence seeking good in the young person's life. This quest for the "not yet" of Laurie's self via the dangerous thicket of its "already," we are reminded, must never compromise deep immersion into painful complexities of her life for the sake of Pollyannish optimism. Instead, while utilizing one's full repertoire of clinical wisdom and skill, the caregiver additionally stands watch for the often subtle advent of an unlikely ally in Laurie's quest for health and transformation, some minuscule passageway through the constricting circumstances of despair, a collaboration unique to every individual case.

With exacting effort Sarah Rand demonstrates the initial complexities of cultivating the soil for this therapeutic accomplice we are calling the eschatological self. Given Laurie's reports of being sexually violated throughout childhood, coupled with her increasing willingness to violate others, Rand faced the delicate task of balancing therapeutic acceptance with appropriate confrontation. Laurie confessed that Rand distinguished herself from previous therapists by taking seriously Laurie's claims to having been raped, likely passing one of Laurie's tests for the conditions of safety and thereby generating rays of hope. Rand also engendered hope by sensitively confronting Laurie's many confusions around boundary issues—evident in Laurie's frank sexual conversations with her father and others, in her sitting too closely to the boys on her unit or giving them her class ring or special goodies from her father, in initiating or responding to overtures for sexual favors, or in daily requests for medical attention. Rand's ethical advocacy regarding the rape investigation, along with these careful confrontations, afforded Laurie safer space when she was incapable of providing herself any such comfortable haven.

Even in the stark severity of her situation, other possible manifestations of Laurie's eschatological self subtly present themselves as well. The fact, for example, that Laurie remained capable of shedding tears during her earliest sessions with Rand likely demonstrated a persevering tenderness of heart that, if nourished, bade well for her future. A caregiver might choose to explore openly, or tuck away for future reference, just what this capacity to cry meant for Laurie. Similarly, Laurie's radiance at recalling childhood days of playing dolls with her aunt and brother in the home of her maternal grandparents leads us to wonder what these memories and relationships mean to her now. I was intrigued, for instance, to learn from Rand that Laurie's aunt, Kelly, attended her exit interview and there explicitly claimed devotion to Christ. And how has Laurie's deceased grandfather, once alcoholic but now her higher power, impacted her own decisions around drugs and alcohol, or her tendencies to worry, appropriately or excessively, about her own physical health? Are Laurie's aunt, brother, or grandparents historically or presently agents of her survival in the throes of her self-destruction? Might they be harbingers of Laurie's eschatological self, holding in trust or doling in palatable portions the self she unconsciously seeks to realize?

These are among countless possible lines of inquiry not far removed from the pain and brokenness of Laurie's life, yet kindled also from remaining embers of her hope and strength. The caregiver should anticipate the surprising fires of *adventus* only after a methodical stoking of *futurum*, including relentless pursuit of even discrete fragments of hope. Any systematic exploration of Laurie's tragic losses and pain must be complemented by consideration of the singularly compelling factors that have conspired for her survival and hope.

Most caregivers are rightly trained to notice therapeutic allies who may be enlisted in the healing process. In addition to Laurie's aunt, grandfather, or brother, any number of other persons or objects may become unexpected agents of decisive transformation: Laurie's father, Carl, perhaps; a cook, custodian, or recreation leader at the group home; her probation officers or health care workers; an adolescent friend; a child or elderly person in her care; or even an unknown stranger on the street. A fascinating array of other relationships or experiences may become instrumental to dramatic change as well: a pet dog or horse, a Barbie doll or a character in a novel or movie, the chance hearing of a song on the radio or a hike at sunrise, a new set of rollerblades or a whitewater rafting expedition. The caregiver in no way can hasten the emergence of any confederate of the eschatological self, nor take much credit for its startling ability to soften previously entrenched patterns. The therapist nevertheless can anticipate, discern, and welcome this agent of hope, strategically enlisting it in the healing task.

In her book *Victimized Daughters: Incest and the Development of the Female Self,* Janet Liebman Jacobs reports that one of her research subjects—an incest victim like Laurie—found such an ally of what we would call her eschatological self in the object of a crucifix. The woman remarked,

> I was on vacation and I walked into this church in California and suddenly I was transfixed by the image of Christ on the cross. I just stared and then I started to cry. Here was this religious symbol that had no real meaning for me—I'm Jewish—and I felt all this emotion. It was the way his body looked, tied to the cross and helpless. That was me, the image of my raped body. Only I had been a young child and here was this adult male, a god, tapping into my unconscious memory. I just cried and cried and I understood why Jesus was such a powerful symbol for the oppressed. I really understood for the first time.[2]

Jacobs reports that identification with Jesus' death on the cross is not uncommon for incest survivors, who frequently liken their experience to victims of the holocaust, fearing invasion by an alien being, by a Nazi soldier, or, for those raised in conservative religious households, by demons or evil spirits.[3] Jacobs found that childhood sexual abuse manifests in symptoms corresponding to post-traumatic stress disorder in combat veterans, involving fear, flashbacks, and sleep disorders: "the victim may have an extreme fear of the dark or of intrusion without knowing who or what is the object of her terror."[4]

Herself such a victim, Laurie is the combat veteran, the holocaust survivor, even the crucified Christ. She hurts herself to feel better, carving her flesh, pulling out her hair, and having sex to remind herself that she is alive. The safety essential to her healing, then, necessarily must surpass even the vast scope of her devastation, a cruciform hope of eschatological proportion.

Rand's interventions and steady progress with Laurie demonstrate that a caregiver can, indeed must, take certain steps to prepare the soil for such hope. We have hinted at additional avenues toward that end worth exploring as well. Further, the caregiver may probe even more directly into the young person's understanding and experiences of God, if such inquiry is tolerated by the youth, or share relevant details of the therapist's own faith or of the story of Jesus itself.

But the severity of Laurie's self-depletion, as well as the nature of God's eschatological workings in the world, demand of her caregivers something *less* as well, that is, something of an unsettling surrender of self. No therapist conjures up God's *adventus* on demand, and when manifested God's presence tends not to differentiate between counselor and counselee in its transformative power. For counselor and young person alike, then, the pastoral relationship becomes one not only of revealing oneself to one another, but of awaiting revelation of oneself *from* the other and, finally, from God. Therapy of this kind is best characterized as an unsettling and imprecise process of mutual thrashing and scanning, of finding and relinquishing the self, of wrestling to discern God's workings of love in the messy singularity of the present predicament, from which neither young person nor caregiver escapes completely unscathed.

If eschatological hope is more like steering a ship in a gale than leisurely drifting in a gondola, then the counseling relationship likely hangs as much upon the severe mercies of God's suffering love in its many unlikely guises, as upon the navigational skill and courage of the caregiver. The eschatological experience of coming to oneself does not necessarily quell the violent storms of self inflicted since childhood upon youth like Laurie, nor those of persons in their wake attempting to help. Recall Rand's own anguish when Laurie ran away from the group home because, as Rand's supervisor put it, "You got close to her"; or Rand's shame and rage as state officials intervened with discharge plans without first consulting her. The currents here run swift, the swells high. But amid so intense a storm, the eschatological self offers assurances of an additional hand on deck, even at ship's helm—no less than that of the same God who raised Jesus from the dead, the historically particular hope to which the eschatological clinician clings. In working with youth like Laurie, this is no small promise.

Chapter Eight

The Case
of Bobby Griffith

*Why did you do this to me, God? Am I going to Hell? That's the gnaw-
ing question that's always drilling little holes in the back of my mind. . . . I
make myself sick. I'm a joke.[1]*

—*Eighteen-year-old Bobby Griffith,*
to his diary

Around midnight on August 27, 1983, twenty-year-old Bobby Griffith—a
blonde, green-eyed, six-feet-tall, muscular, "tousle-haired Tom Sawyer"[2]—
performed a backflip from an overpass twenty-five feet above the main interstate freeway in downtown Portland, Oregon, into the path of an
oncoming tractor-trailer. The driver tried to swerve, but to no avail. Bobby's
body was thrown fourteen feet, his clothing ripped from his body, and his
life instantly taken. Witnesses to the leap initially thought it was a prank. It
was, instead, the culmination of years of Bobby's failed attempts to reconcile
his Christian faith with his sexual orientation.

What served as the final act in Bobby's long struggle for meaning in the
face of his yearnings for other men was only the beginning of a related, yet
quite different search for meaning for Bobby's mother, Mary Griffith. His
death inaugurated for her a relentless quest for assurance that her son was
with God and that she would see him again in eternal life, a quest that finally
took her to a destination she scarcely could have imagined at the outset.

The following case study is taken from Leroy Aarons's biographical account of Bobby Griffith and his mother in his book *Prayers for Bobby: A
Mother's Coming to Terms with the Suicide of Her Gay Son.* Aarons weaves the
story of Bobby's daily struggle with his sexuality, chronicled in compelling
diaries that Bobby kept for four years prior to his death, with his mother's
unflinching account of her own dramatic conversion on her pilgrimage for
peace in the wake of her son's tragic demise.

"Dear God: Are You There?
I Ask Because I Really Don't Know"

In May 1979, fifteen-year-old Bobby Griffith could no longer sustain the terrible burden of his secret alone and in desperation chose his older brother, Ed, then seventeen, as confidant. An athletic youth with dreams of becoming a professional baseball player, Ed was in many ways Bobby's opposite. Yet the boys were close, sharing a devout Christian faith as well as a bedroom since childhood, every now and then curling up in each other's arms at night in their bunk beds.[3]

The brothers, now adolescents, lay near an apricot tree in the backyard of Bob and Mary Griffith's modest 1940s-era tract home in Walnut Creek, California, just east of San Francisco Bay. Bobby began by telling Ed, "There's something awful I have to tell you. You are going to really hate me and never want to talk to me again." After receiving reassurance of Ed's love, Bobby blurted out, "I'm gay." When Ed asked whether Bobby had told their parents, Bobby grew hostile, demanding that Ed not reveal their secret to anyone. Ed promised but at a significant cost to his own peace of mind, for, to him, homosexuality "was like something from another planet."[4] Revealing his secret to Ed also failed to release Bobby as he had hoped from his increasing depression. Weeks later, just prior to his sixteenth birthday, he wrote in his diary:

> Dear God: Are you there? I ask because I really don't know. . . . Sometimes I hurt so bad, and I'm scared and alone. I wonder why you or somebody doesn't help. I'm so mad and frustrated, I seem to be at the end of the road. Why do you remain silent?[5]

Ed's alarm at Bobby's despair grew, and when Bobby confessed that he had recently swallowed half of a bottle of aspirin, Ed became afraid for his brother's life and decided to tell their mother that Bobby was gay. When she heard, Mary assured Ed that God could handle this: "God will help us, and he will heal Bobby." Mary, in turn, proceeded to tell her husband, Bob, a union electrician and the only member of the family besides Bobby's youngest sister, Nancy, uninterested in the Christian faith at the center of the rest of the family's life. Later that evening Mary and Bob confronted Bobby, who in turn was horrified that his secret was out. He stormed from the room. His mother followed him to his room, where he told her through his tears that he had always felt this way: "Other guys dream of girls. I dream of men. And I enjoy it!"[6] Mary sought to comfort Bobby by telling him she had seen on television that with God's help homosexuality was "curable" and that God would help him "weed it out." They talked until 4 A.M., with Bobby desperately wanting to believe that his mother was right.

"I Seriously Wonder
If I'll Live to Be Very Old"

That night confirmed for Mary Griffith a suspicion she secretly had har-
bored since Bobby's early childhood—a sense that her son was "different."
Bobby had been a scrawny child of gentle spirit, almost too good and too
obedient for Mary. He was not a roughhousing boy, instead opting to play
indoors with stuffed animals, dolls, and his mother's jewelry. He attended
to the intricate details of nature. At age three or four, Bobby dressed up in
his sister's slip and started kissing and hugging some neighbor boys. Their
distressed mother phoned to inform Mary of Bobby's behavior. When he
gleefully returned home, Mary tore off the slip and reprimanded him never
to get into his sister's things again.

She redoubled her efforts to discourage all things feminine in her
youngest son; when at age five he asked for a doll for Christmas, she
bought him a "masculine" pretend shaver instead. Ed, one year ahead of
Bobby in school, likewise sought, without success, to teach his brother
how to play baseball. "You throw like a girl," Ed would yell in frustration. When at a parent-teacher conference Mary learned from his teacher
that Bobby preferred to play with the girls, Mary felt "intimidated" and
distraught. Years later, she would notice that Bobby, at age thirteen,
would sit mesmerized in front of the television morning and evening
watching fitness guru Jack LaLanne, yet without ever performing the exercise routines himself.[7]

Before entering puberty, Bobby seemed a happy, free-spirited boy. He
organized backyard carnivals for neighborhood children, loved animals,
and won essay prizes for his writing skills. He was shy, but mildly mischie-
vous, and loved to laugh. At puberty, however, Bobby came face-to-face
with the fact that his yearnings had a label, and his quiet, loving, childhood
demeanor shifted to despondent melancholy. He often heard his maternal
grandmother, Ophelia, remark of gay people, "They should line 'em up
against a wall and shoot 'em."[8] Now, at age sixteen, Bobby could no longer
deny that he was among those denounced by his grandmother; only then
did he first voice himself the words his mother had so long feared. Mary's
suspicions could no longer be suppressed.

Upon Bobby's revelation Mary found what seemed a mission from God
for her life, that of delivering her son from his affliction. Along with Ed,
her most spiritually devout child, Mary searched out books on homosexuality from the library and their church bookstore, all of which shared
Mary's own view that homosexuality was a distortion of God's intention
for creation. She took Bobby to a Christian psychologist recommended by
their pastor at Walnut Creek Presbyterian Church, where the Griffiths
long had been actively involved. She placed Bible verses targeted for Bobby

around their home, including on the bathroom mirror. She turned up the volume on the Christian radio station so that Bobby would overhear. She prayed over him in his room at night as he slept. Her message was singularly focused: Bobby "had to trust God to heal him, and [understand] that Satan would try to discourage him."[9]

For his part, Bobby himself was terrified by prospects of falling victim to Satan's grip and burning in hell, and so read his Bible and prayed dutifully. Outside observers of the family during this period saw the Griffiths "crucifying" Bobby with their religious excoriations, often well into the night—what one of Bobby's friends described as a "hammering away, the chiseling of his soul." In his only diary entry of 1980, Bobby wrote, "At the rate I'm going now . . . I seriously wonder if I'll live to be very old, that is if I will live past being a teenager."[10]

"I've Chosen Sin over Righteousness"

Over the course of four years before his death, and with the exception of a sole entry for all of 1980, Bobby regularly recorded his most personal thoughts in his diaries. Following his suicide, the four notebooks were returned to his mother and, in opening and beginning to read them several days after his funeral, Mary learned for the first time the extent of her son's inner agony. There Bobby, who at age ten told his mother that he wanted to accept Christ into his life and was then baptized, wrote pleading prayers to God for deliverance from his sexual turmoil:

> Why did you do this to me, God? Am I going to Hell? That's the gnawing question that's always drilling little holes in the back of my mind. . . . I make myself sick. I'm a joke.[11]

Or again:

> The anger never erupts. . . . My timid nature would never allow a full fledged thunder storm to occur, but it is there, looming quietly on the horizon. . . . I can feel God's eyes looking down on me with such pity. He can't help me though, because I've chosen sin over righteousness.[12]

But his anger did find outlet in his journals, and along with self-scathing prayers, Mary also found in them rage-filled blasphemies. Just before his eighteenth birthday, Bobby wrote,

> I think I only write when I'm depressed. Right now I just want to die, just die. . . . I sit here groveling and wonder who in the fuck is up there watching. Is there anyone? I really doubt it. Sometimes I get so mad I feel like I could just scream loud enough for God to hear me: "What in the fuck do

you think you're doing sitting on your ass just watching the damn mess you created down here?" But I guess it just echoes around, bouncing from cloud to cloud unheard by anyone.[13]

The diaries revealed that Bobby had his first sexual experience at age seventeen with a man he met at a grocery store. Soon other men would call him, and he began to disappear for weekends. Mary felt the need to increase the pressure by telling him that he wasn't trying or praying hard enough, that he needed more faith. Angry and rebellious, just weeks prior to graduation Bobby dropped out of high school.

He found a monotonous job assembling picture frames, started lifting weights to improve his sexual attractiveness, and felt his way into the myriad possibilities of San Francisco's gay night life. But he had no lasting friendships or intimate relationships, and his mood alternated between decadent grandiosity and writhing self-contempt. A gay high school teacher introduced Bobby to another gay student, Mark Guyere, at his former school. They went to a movie and then to a park and, for a moment, Bobby uncharacteristically lifted his emotional shield, sharing with Mark his religious dilemma, his mother's moralistic tactics, and about a time, Mark remembered, when Mary told Bobby to burn his Bible. Mark, an agnostic, found Bobby's demeanor and story to be

> unbearably sad and incomprehensible. [Mark] could not remember ever seeing anyone hurting so badly. It was in Bobby's face, in the way he talked. It was clear that the most important thing to Bobby was that God love him.[14]

Other friends at that time saw in Bobby excessive concern for approval from everyone around him. He seemed to care too much about what others thought of him. They saw his life rocketing out of control, as Bobby raced from scene to scene, from work to home to the theater to the gym to gay night at the skating rink to the sex arcades of San Francisco. Mary, however, misread Bobby's deepening irritability and despair as a sign that her interventions on his behalf were working. The more deeply he sank into depression, the nearer she believed him to being cured of his homosexuality and convicted and released from his sin.[15]

Shortly after his nineteenth birthday, Bobby quit his job and, weeks later, became a prostitute for several months, making enough money to pay off some loans and give money to his mother. But his life as a "male model" only increased Bobby's self-loathing. Things were growing more unsettled at home as well. The Griffiths' four children—Joy, then age twenty-two, Ed at twenty-one, Bobby at nineteen, and younger sister, Nancy, thirteen—all remained living in their parents' home. Bobby despised living there, and for endless hours would shut himself into a makeshift private bedroom that he had carved for himself from a small attic loft.

By late summer of 1982, a fight erupted one day when Ed told Bobby to stop teasing Nancy. Bobby persisted, and Ed exploded. A fist fight and wrestling match ensued between the brothers, which carried over into other rooms of the house. At one point Bobby, with newly realized physical strength, picked up his athletic older brother and threw him across their sisters' bedroom. Shocking himself at this, Bobby rushed into the bathroom, sobbing. Ed followed him there and apologized, but Bobby brushed past him back into his sisters' room, where he smashed his fist into a mirror on their door, shattering the glass. Ed rushed in to help. Bobby cried out to him, "All I ever wanted was to be like you!" Ed's own response surprised him: "That's funny. I've wanted to be like you! You've got the good looks, the height, and all the girls think you're really neat."[16]

Shortly after this explosive incident, Bobby's favorite cousin, Jeanette, herself a lesbian, invited Bobby to live with her and her partner in Portland. He pondered this invitation for months, even as his depression continued to mount, exacerbated by an unsuccessful surgical dermabrasion of his severe facial acne scars. In a diary entry dated January 4, 1983, Bobby wrote,

> Everyone around here is under the impression that all I have to do is surrender my life to Jesus Christ. It's that simple. But they can't see that it's not. . . . It's an awful feeling to believe that one is headed straight to fires of hell. What makes everything worse is having all these people around you telling you how simple the solution is when it doesn't really seem to be at all. . . . [17]

It was Bobby's mother who, upon returning home one day to find Bobby kicking the tires of his car in rage, finally suggested that, given his unhappiness, Bobby consider moving to Portland. On February 7, he boarded a bus and, with excitement tainted by Mary's deep ambivalence over his leaving, was bound for Portland.

"My Life Is Over As Far As I'm Concerned"

Portland represented a new beginning for Bobby, and initially he seemed to thrive there. He loved his cousin Jeanette and was welcomed into their home by her companion. He got a couple of minimum-wage jobs, began to exercise again, and swore off sex for the sake of sex alone. He revealed to his cousin that he had never had sex with someone for whom he cared, and that he longed to know from her what that was like.[18]

His initial celibacy did not last long, however, and after Bobby stayed away for an entire weekend without informing Jeanette of his whereabouts, she became concerned and asked him to move out of her home. He moved across town into the home of another cousin, Debbie. His diary indicated how devastating Jeanette's disapproval was for him.

The spring initially seemed to bring renewed hope. In June, he told his diary, "The pen I'm writing with says, 'For with God nothing shall be impossible.' Luke 1:37. I think it's true." Yet one month later, he wrote, "My life is over as far as I'm concerned."[19] Bobby was scheduled for a five-day vacation at home in California around the end of July. His parents met him at the airport, and Mary was shocked at her son's appearance. Even his breathing seemed effortful. While Bobby never wrote about AIDS in his diary, both he and Mary feared the disease, and Bobby seemed resigned to becoming its victim. At home in California his spirits seemed to alternate between lethargy and hair-trigger sensitivity.

He returned to Portland following this brief break, this time without emotional good-bye hugs for his family. He resumed work and, to his deep satisfaction, managed to repair the damaged relationship with Jeanette. In his last journal entry, written after an all-night dancing spree with her, Bobby referred to Jeanette as his "very best friend." He pasted her picture there. One week later, on August 26, he asked his cousin Debbie if she would buy him a bottle of liquor, since he was underage. She found this a strange request, given that Bobby usually did not drink, and she refused to oblige him. That evening, Bobby headed downtown toward the gay bar section. Hours later, at 12:30 A.M., a driver and passenger who were stopped at a red light watched Bobby walk alone across the interstate overpass. Within seconds, he leapt over the railing to his death.[20]

"I Thought You Were a Loving Father"

Bobby's funeral was held at Walnut Creek Presbyterian Church, a conservative congregation whose pastors publicly condemned their denomination's wrestling with questions concerning homosexuality. At the funeral, Bobby's family heard the young minister tell the congregation that homosexuality is a sin and, out of deep "frustration" and "disillusionment" with that "lifestyle," Bobby had chosen to take his life. But the pastor also assured the congregation that Bobby had accepted Christ and, despite the sins of homosexuality and suicide, nothing could separate a Christian from the love of God. Bobby's place in God's kingdom was secure.

Mary, however, was not so sure. The thought that she might never see her son in eternal life shook the foundations of her faith. Why had her project to heal Bobby failed so miserably? How could it have turned out like this? Why had God not brought the deliverance for which she had so long prayed? Mary kept her troubling questions hidden, knowing that if she were to raise them her pastors would only reassure her of Bobby's salvation. But according to her own reading of the scriptures, she feared that Bobby must now be in hell.[21]

In the days and weeks that followed, the family remained in a dazed stupor of grief. Joy found herself crying in the car each day on her way to work. Ed decided not to register for college classes and would sometimes remain in bed for days at a time. Nancy worried that it could happen to her, that she could "turn gay." Bob lamented that he had underestimated the depth of his son's pain, and Mary began to blame him for not trying harder to help Bobby. Their sex life fell to zero. Strikingly, Mary would not let herself surrender to her own beliefs concerning God's judgment of her son's soul, even though her challenges to God bordered on blasphemy in her mind.[22]

Within months, Mary quit her job as a department store shipping clerk and stopped attending Walnut Creek Presbyterian. She shut herself up in a makeshift study in a utility room of her home and began searching the scriptures for answers to her questions. She sought to revisit what the Bible said about homosexuality. Mary confided in Ed, who began to notice changes in her; she no longer spewed forth scriptural answers as in the past, but now seemed the student, the seminarian in search of answers. She began writing restless letters to God, not unlike those in Bobby's diaries: "You could have given Bobby something or someone to hang onto, but you didn't, and you don't for a lot of people." Sixteen months after his death, Mary still remained disquieted concerning his soul. She wrote to God: "I thought you were a loving Father. I'm not so sure anymore." And with this, as suddenly as she had begun, Mary suspended writing her pleading tomes to God.[23]

Distraught that the Bible could not confirm for her Bobby's place in God's plan of creation, Mary began reading a book that Bobby had once given her but that she had never opened. It was entitled *Loving Someone Gay*, by psychologist Don Clark. She read:

> Once upon a time, people selected the most beautiful and talented youths of the community and ceremoniously threw them into boiling volcanoes as an offering to appease the angry gods. . . . Some parents are still willing to sacrifice their beautiful gay offspring to appease the god of conformity. . . . [Their children's] act of self-murder is a shame that we who represent the society must bear.[24]

These words led Mary to wonder for the first time whether she had misunderstood Bobby's situation from the very beginning and whether Bobby may have been right to assert his gay sexuality all along. About this time,

Mary had a dream in which Bobby kept directing her to a book that, when she read from it, said, "God is all goodness." Mary awoke to consider that if God is all goodness, then God could not do every terrible thing that the Bible said God does. God was not against Bobby. She returned to the Bible once again, now discovering more and more passages that she could no longer read as literal truth.[25]

Mary concluded that she had journeyed as far into her critical analysis of the Bible as she could on her own. She knew that she needed expert theological help. In the throes of a powerful transformation in her mind, in which now, rather than condemning her son's homosexuality, she wanted to validate it, she remembered a nearby Metropolitan Community Church that ministered primarily to gay and lesbian persons. She phoned its pastor, who met and talked with her over the course of several hours about Bobby and, more to her longing, about her questions regarding scriptural interpretation. He told Mary about critical methods of biblical interpretation and of alternate ways that scholars understand the handful of texts that refer to homosexuality in the Bible. Mary was stunned. Following their conversation, she grew increasingly intrigued and emboldened to make several more appointments with the pastor. Eventually, she agreed to attend worship there, where she was surprised to find a joyous fellowship of Christians. She became animated and excited, the transformation of her understanding unfolding at a breathtaking pace.[26]

Finally, the pastor asked Mary if she had heard of a national organization called P-FLAG, an acronym for Parents, Family, and Friends of Lesbians and Gays. He arranged for her to meet with Betty Lambert, another mother of a gay son, and together they began to drive to various P-FLAG meetings throughout the Bay area. Although it took her some time to work up the courage to speak at these meetings, eventually Mary began to open up. She told her story to hushed and affirming listeners who inevitably were moved by the compelling simplicity of her presentation and its message of guilt and grief over the loss of Bobby. Eventually, her story was retold in a San Francisco newspaper and then drew national attention. The introverted, unpolished, working-class mother found herself repeatedly telling her story on national television and around the country as a national representative of P-FLAG.[27]

As Mary opened herself to these various new learnings and experiences, she would return home to process them, especially with Ed, himself increasingly unsettled with his own religious understandings. Ed was receptive to his mother's new ideas but would be rebuffed when he presented them to others at Walnut Creek Presbyterian. One of the ministers there told him that Mary was simply reinterpreting scripture as a means of coping with her own guilt over Bobby's suicide. But the pastor's comments were not convincing to Ed, who began to drift away from the church.

For her part, Mary finally received the peace she sought concerning Bobby. She remembered a dream of hers shortly after his death, in which Bobby was laughing heartily. She asked in disbelief, "Bobby, is that you?" He replied, "Why shouldn't it be?" And she was thrilled that he was alive. Mary became certain, years later, that the meaning of this dream was the answer to her search: "[God] had not healed Bobby *because there was nothing wrong with him.*"[28]

The New Creation as Re-Creation

We notice in beginning to reflect on this case that Bobby Griffith clearly shares many of the prominent attributes of the endangered self: dramatic narcissistic mood swings from grandiose self-entitlement to melancholic self-loathing; fits of rage coupled with intense shame and interpersonal isolation; extreme difficulty in reconciling his own self experience with expectations of his family, including an exaggerated attachment to and resentment of his mother, exacerbated by an apparently wide emotional gulf between Bobby and his father; and increasingly self-destructive forms of behavioral acting out, evident in his disappearing on weekends, in sexual promiscuity and eventual prostitution, and in quitting high school only weeks before graduation.

Bobby's case distinguishes itself as well from those of Stan, John Turner, and Laurie, certainly in his explicit struggle with sexual orientation, but also in his conscious and agonizing quest for communion with God and in the finally prevailing despair of his tragic death. His story demonstrates how high are the stakes in therapeutic interventions with young people in crisis, and it exposes the vacuity of previously reigning and in some cases still lingering myths of professional neutrality in clinical work. The nature of Bobby's dilemmas implores caregivers, pastoral or otherwise, to enter a hornet's nest of political and ecclesial controversy, to challenge their culture's willingness to sacrifice young people to the appetites of often anonymous idols of church and society.

Because Bobby's desperation centers in issues of his faith, it poses particular concerns for pastoral caregivers. Theological miscalculations escalate here into deadly perils, summoning theologically credentialed clinicians back from exile at the fringes of the therapeutic disciplines. For its many compelling psychological, familial, and sociocultural dynamics, Bobby's predicament virtually begs for nuanced theological conversation at the table of contemporary clinical care, a discourse many healing professionals remain ill at ease to initiate or sustain.

Bobby's high school friend, Mark Guyere, observed that what Bobby desired most was for God to love him, a love, we surmise, not just blithely proclaimed to him by another but needing also to be demonstrated biblically and intellectually and embodied interpersonally. Bobby's surrendering his life to Christ—which he attempted to do—was not enough. Neither were immersions in a panoply of sexual options, nor even a treasured relationship with his beloved cousin, Jeanette. The sharp distinctions drawn between Bobby's sensitive faith and his sexual orientation needed somehow to be bridged and transcended, with neither faith nor sexuality slighted in the process. But given that these same dichotomies penetrated his close circles of intimates, including his family, church, and gay and lesbian acquaintances, and permeated the wider culture as well, Bobby's chances for identifying any priestly mediator of change appeared remote. Who could provide him the therapeutic conditions of safety, the joyful sadness of a happy ending that incorporated both Bobby's essential Christian faith and his defining sexual orientation? Where is the eschatological self needed to perforate and redeem his constricted future and journey into despair?

If our construct of self is bounded solely by the historical period of Bobby's time on earth from birth to death, then questions such as these would linger to trouble us with meaninglessness and despair. But if the self is conceived eschatologically—as held in trust, in part, by others and ultimately by God in Christ—then even the parameters of Bobby's birth and death, however significant for the life of the self, cannot finally determine or contain him. Indeed, Bobby's story presses us toward this latter conclusion, given its clear indications that his untimely death tragically interrupts but never fully annihilates his presence or mission. Bobby's eschatological self continues to impact especially his mother after his death, not only through her memories of him or by means of his diaries but, even more directly, in his contacting her through dreams at once disturbing and comforting. Without Mary's attempting to conjure him up, Bobby keeps appearing to her, suggesting a self somehow more encompassing than one constructed solely historically or culturally. While we remain intrigued concerning the possibility of the eschatological self's preceding even one's birth, Bobby's story, at the very least, makes a compelling case for the life of the self following death.

Some people of faith will feel more at ease considering such claims in terms of the familiar language of "spirit" or "soul," rich words certainly worth retaining in our theological vocabulary. But by extending the concept of self beyond even the boundaries of life and death, we intensify the eschatological conviction that God in Christ makes all things, including the self, new, in such a way discontinuous with yet without destroying the old. Moltmann, for example, writes that

> [j]ust as the raised Christ does not *develop* out of the crucified and dead Christ, the *novum ultimum*—the ultimate new thing—does not *issue* from

the history of the old. . . . The new thing is the surprising thing, the thing that could never have been expected. It evokes unbounded astonishment, and transforms the people whom it touches.

Yet even the eschatological "new thing" is not without analogy. If it were completely incomparable . . . it would be impossible to say anything about it at all. What is eschatologically new, itself creates its own continuity, since it does not annihilate the old but gathers it up and creates it anew. . . . The raised Christ is the crucified Christ and no other, but he is the crucified Christ in transfigured form (Phil. 3:21). The coming God is not *Deus novus*, a new God. . . . He is the God who *is faithful to his creation*.[29]

The "new" Bobby Griffith, who with warm laughter and assurances of God's goodness comes to his mother in astonishing dreams, remains irrevocably bound up with the old Bobby, who pleaded with God in his abandonment and despair. The new creation of Bobby's eschatological self gathers up and *re*-creates his developing, embodied, historical self, which, without diminishing the tragedy of his death, gives us pause to wonder and hope.

Eschatological Selves

We notice as well in this story how closely allied is the advent of Bobby's eschatological self with that of his mother. In Mary we witness nothing short of a remarkable psychosocial and spiritual transformation in the aftermath of her son's death, the result, in part, of her own dogged search for answers to viscerally wrenching questions concerning the state of Bobby's, and likely her own, soul. Mary's strivings are balanced, too, by a vulnerable surrender of self to alternative new voices: to the writing of psychologist Don Clark, or the voices of the pastor of the Metropolitan Community Church or P-FLAG mother Betty Lambert, but, more strikingly, to a poignant voice within, as Mary's own dreams guided her to trust Bobby's message that God is all goodness or to find reassurance of her son's laughter in death. Bobby's death empowered, even coerced, Mary to embrace and suffer the advent of her eschatological self—a woman now less fearful to question previously entrenched beliefs or sanctioned authorities, one more critically and thoughtfully attuned to the biblical witness, one surmounting timidity and shame to share her tragic testimony with others— all of this change occurring, it felt to her, with breathtaking rapidity.

Mary's pastor at Walnut Creek Presbyterian dismissed these changes, contending that they merely betrayed Mary's guilt and denial concerning Bobby's death. While ample support for this pastor's interpretation could be conjured in most churches and the culture at large, I side with Mary and Ed in considering implausible the pastor's rendering of Mary's transformation. Was she defending herself from suffering by quitting her job, holing herself up in a makeshift study, poring over the scriptures and other literature, journaling, praying, questioning, dreaming, and seeking counsel from those with viewpoints conflicting with her own? Might not these actions be interpreted, rather, as signs of an uncharacteristic lowering of her defenses and an opening of self to realistic or necessary suffering?

Certainly Mary's new self-understanding *increased* her suffering exponentially, given that, for the first time, she perceived and accepted with grievous horror her own role in her son's suicide. Contrary to her pastor's explanation, Mary's new perspective in no way shielded her from guilt but pressed her more deeply into it, moving her to acknowledge complicity in Bobby's death, while finding in this shameful embrace not only a harrowing cross but also a redemptive hope. She experienced this astonishing revelation as a joyful sadness, a satisfying release of pent-up anguish, and a severe mercy that propelled her to face more unflinchingly her pain and grief and, equally striking, to enter into increasingly complex contradictions in society as a national spokesperson for P-FLAG. This new Mary is somehow much less prone to denial than her pastor suggests, yet she herself was as surprised as any by these changes in and around her. She appears a less caricatured, more expansive person by the end of the story, an empowered prophet, energized and enriching others for having encountered her eschatological self.

Mary Griffith's newfound conclusion—that Bobby's sexual orientation was ordained and blessed by God—appears irreconcilable with the perspective of her former pastors and church. Precipitating a flood of self-examination in his mother's life, Bobby's suicide spurs no perceptible ripple of personal or theological introspection among his pastors or congregation. These latter, of course, are buttressed on this matter by centuries of church history and tradition, by a smattering of condemnatory biblical texts, and by the still current, if ambivalent, official policies of their larger Presbyterian Church (U.S.A.) and most other denominational bodies.

Against this formidable array, must not the church be reminded that it, too, awaits its eschatological self, a clearer glimpse of the church as God intends it, in the longed-for coming of Christ? Even while proclaiming to others the "already" and "not yet" paradox of its faith, the institutional church sometimes spares itself immersion into this unsettling mystery. Like individuals in crisis, the church under duress is prone to defer to previous sensibilities rather than explore the less familiar theological terrain evoked by a gay youth's suicide. Such retreat, of course, is a natural and sometimes even prudent response, given the wisdom found in much of the church's history and tradition.

When locked, however, into this backward glance, cut off from eschatological promise, the church's institutional self comes to mimic the abandonment depression and pathological narcissism of youth whose selves are similarly bereft of future hope. Like young people unwilling or unable to sustain realistic suffering for the sake of right relationships, the disparaging or depleted church concentrates instead on its present survival or growth, likely displacing its own requisite suffering on dispossessed others.

The eschatologically accessible church, by contrast, cannot afford to bask in any assurance that its previous understandings or practices reign exhaustive; its theology instead must function, to borrow the expression of Charles M. Wood, as "an aspect of the continuing repentance" of the church.[30] The church that awaits the coming of God must continuously adjudicate fierce and conflicting centrifugal and centripetal pressures, steering its ship in a gale, attempting to focus on Christ. Its hope cannot sidestep even its own cruciform demise, the church, too, a seed that falls into the earth and dies.

Within a hundred years after Pentecost, early Christians already had abandoned or altered three of the foundational pillars of their Jewish heritage—the regulations dictating circumcision, dietary rituals, and the day on which the Sabbath was to be observed—although none of these without intense controversy and struggle. Church history is strewn with countless other such volatile reversals. We later Christians are left to determine whether the despair of Bobby Griffith and young people in similar predicaments bespeaks their apostasy or their martyrdom, whether heretical abomination or creative theological breakthrough.[31]

Although anything is possible, it remains difficult to envision any heterosexual young people committing suicide as a result of the church throwing wide its doors to homosexual persons. Yet evidence mounts that gay and lesbian youths continue to take their own lives as those doors stand closed.[32] If Christ's resurrection was orchestrated by a God of life, not death, then would that this observation alone lead the church to question its prevalent policies on sexual orientation. But like Mary Griffith before her son's death, and most others of us still, the church will not likely suffer gladly its eschatological self, perpetuating instead the loss of its sensitive youth.

Epilogue: Awaiting

Those who wait for the Lord shall renew their strength.
> *—Isaiah 40:31a*

We are not ourselves, although we are becoming ourselves, and in rare moments of joyful sadness or severe mercy we come to ourselves. We meet ourselves coming and going.

The frequently formidable tensions between becoming and coming, autonomy and surrender, gradual development and astonishing breakthrough, human struggle and divine initiative, historical embodiment and eternal re-creation, *futurum* and *adventus,* and cross and resurrection together comprise the eschatological self. This self enjoys no leisurely drifting in a Venetian gondola but rather steers its ship in a gale.

For one given to tasks of aiding troubled young people who, by most indications, find themselves increasingly depleted and vulnerable, conceiving of the self eschatologically can supply hope amid the confusion. Since we are not ourselves, but receive the self, in part, from others—on occasion from a stranger or chance encounter, more often from those on whom we most depend, and ultimately from the God who has hidden our life with Christ—then no current construction of self can finally determine or delimit our future. However grounded in present concerns, the eschatological self holds forth hope that the best is yet to be. Who dares to say that the God whose only work is love cannot redeem even the tragedy of one's current circumstance or the terrible abandonment of troubled youth? Who knows what adventure of self God yet holds in store?

Bonding with Your Paperboy

A nightly ritual called, simply, "Story" made a lasting impression on me during a Clinical Pastoral Education residency in an adolescent psychiatric hospital some years ago. Every evening around bedtime, boys and girls separated by that hour, hospital staff workers would choose and read a short story to the patients. For twenty or thirty minutes the youth would listen quietly as an attendant read aloud to them.

Given their daytime propensity to challenge nearly every other component of their treatment regimens, the young people's relative lack of protest concerning a bedtime story struck me as significant. I found it odd that they appeared content to endure, even to enjoy, hearing a story each night. Yet my surprise was tempered by recalling high school church camps where even the oldest youth appreciated hearing stories read by their cabin counselors. That emotionally troubled and relatively healthy youth alike welcomed such rituals spoke to me not only of the power of stories, but also of the peculiar station in life of the young person, at once the little child delighting in a good yarn, yet also the earnest novice absorbing whatever might afford entrance into the prized freedom of adulthood.

Recalling this storytelling ritual in the ensuing years has often given me pause to reconsider when I am tempted to equate the sheer physical stature of young people with their emotional or spiritual maturity, or when I find myself intimidated into standing my distance by their style of dress or attitude of apparent nonchalance. I am reminded that youths remain in need of relationships with adults, however increasingly difficult such interaction is to instigate or maintain. For adults today to engage in even casual conversation with a young person, particularly one exuding callous indifference, takes a certain measure of courage and an even greater degree of perseverance. Our orbits appear culturally contrived never to intersect. "It takes effort to bond with your paperboy," quips therapist Mary Pipher,[1] and when your paperboy, or papergirl, is among the increasing number of profoundly troubled youth, that effort is multiplied in intensity.

Such intensive involvement with youth in the process of becoming a self, we have seen, is necessary for providing the requisite conditions of safety, the vital soil, for enhancing their stewardship of pain and engendering seeds of eschatological hope. This hope insists that caregivers draw upon the full wealth of practical wisdom of the human sciences, including, but not limited to, the developmental psychologies considered here. It presses us further to advocate for justice on behalf of youth in diverse family, civic, and corporate arenas. Eschatological hope never legitimately disengages from the harsh paradoxes of individual, interpersonal, and institutional living and dying; it sustains active interest in the young person's unique struggle of becoming in relation to self, others, and God.

Pastoral caregivers and other concerned adults must, by their own intentional initiatives, court relationships with troubled youth in order to effect needed change. We must steel our courage to penetrate young people's seemingly impervious facades and thereby elicit their concerns and stories. We must learn to expect and tolerate at times our own envy of their vulnerability and candor, as well as anticipate their challenging tests for the conditions of safety. Perhaps most difficult, we need to trust, against all appearances, their desire to hear our own sacred convictions. It takes effort to bond with your paperboy, and even more to open youth in crisis to the *futurum* of eschatological hope.

Eschatological Patience

The foregoing cases of Stan, John Turner, Laurie, and Bobby Griffith point as well to the frustrations experienced by those adults who attempt to help. While it remains possible to envision satisfying resolutions to these cases, what prevails instead are their more uncertain endings. None of the caregivers who intervened received any assurances that his or her efforts finally made a difference; none likely will see whether his or her work has borne fruit.

These ambiguous outcomes point to the fact that working with troubled youths requires not only intentional effort but also a kind of surrender, an unusual sort of patience, beyond that even ordinarily demanded for assisting difficult persons. The constraints of not knowing, often of never knowing, the results of our toils with young people necessitate patience of eschatological proportion, a willingness to trust beyond sight and certitude the value of our efforts on their behalf. Eschatological patience involves hoping *against* hope, against all appearances to the contrary that these youth remain worthy of advocacy even when our well-intended intervention goes awry. Such patience stems from a source beyond any historical contingency or human achievement, originating, rather, in the eschatological promises of God demonstrated pivotally "under Pontius Pilate."

Every caregiver seeks to effect changes through his or her courage, insight, and therapeutic skill; but the pastoral counselor embracing eschatological hope anticipates and relies on an additional power for healing beyond any achievement of his or her own, beyond, finally, even the threat of death itself. That this eschatological transformation centers in the cross of Christ demands persistent pastoral entrance into the ambiguity and fray of the lives of young people, drawing eagerly from contemporary psychology and other relevant disciplines. That this transformation is experienced finally as a gift more than an accomplishment, that it gathers up and reveals an astonishing newness of self to caregiver and young person alike, speaks to our dependency on God's presence to sustain ministry with troubled youth. Like the risen Christ's appearances to his disciples, the *adventus* solution—the eschatological patience, trust, and hope— comes as a surprise, when it comes at all, to those who discipline themselves for the search.

In his book *The Presence of God in Pastoral Counseling*, pastoral theologian Wayne Oates reminds his readers that "God's Presence does not keep a therapeutic schedule at the beck and call of a pastoral counselor," but also that the "hungering darkness" of God's absence often serves as the very prelude to healing:

> In this sense, pastoral counseling itself becomes prayer. . . . You wait.
>
> You pray that you may not weary of [the one you counsel]. You are gripped by your own finiteness, your own weariness. You shift into quiet listening, as far as the counselee can see. It is an intense, petitioning kind of prayer before God, from your standpoint. You wait upon the Lord that both your and the counselee's strength may be renewed. You ask that energy and hope will be provided for the time at hand and until you see them again.[2]

The cases of Stan, John Turner, Laurie, and Bobby Griffith show that our awaiting the coming of God, who bears us to ourselves, intensifies disproportionately in working with youth in crisis, and frequently evolves into an endless awaiting, an eternal unknowing, an eschatological ambiguity of prayer. Attempting at all so uncertain a task witnesses to a hope against hope that, in life and in death, we belong to God, and that, when all is said and done, youth and pastors together will find in Christ an ending so happy, there won't be a dry eye in the house.

Notes

Introduction

1. Paul C. Holinger, Daniel Offer, James T. Barter, Carl C. Bell, *Suicide and Homicide among Adolescents* (New York: Guilford Press, 1994), 43, 50, 52, 93.

2. Fox Butterfield, "Teen-Age Homicide Rate Has Soared," *New York Times*, 14 October 1994, 10(A).

3. Eloise Salholz with Gregory Cerio, "Short Lives, Bloody Deaths: Black Murder Rates Soar," *Newsweek*, 17 December 1990, 33.

4. Fox Butterfield, "More Blacks in Their 20's Have Trouble with the Law," *New York Times*, 5 October 1995, 8(A).

5. Susan G. Millstein and Iris F. Litt, "Adolescent Health," in *At the Threshold: The Developing Adolescent*, ed. S. Shirley Feldman and Glen R. Elliott (Cambridge: Harvard University Press, 1990), 433–34.

6. Jane E. Brody, "Teen-Agers' Accidents May Be Warnings of Suicide," *New York Times*, 24 March 1993, 7(B).

7. The U.S. poverty line in 1989 was $12,675 for a family of four. See the report by the National Association of State Boards of Education, *Code Blue: Uniting for Healthier Youth* (1012 Cameron St., Alexandria, VA 22314), 2; and Tom Morganthau et al., "Losing Ground," *Newsweek*, 6 April 1992, 20; and U.S. Department of Education, *Youth Indicators 1991* (Washington, D.C.: U.S. Government Printing Office, April 1991), 38–39.

8. "Youth Health Still Declining in America, Study Says," *New York Times*, 7 June 1995, 16(A); Millstein and Litt, "Adolescent Health" in Feldman and Elliott, *At the Threshold*, 435; U.S. Department of Education, *Code Blue*, 2; and Daniel Goldman, "Teen-Agers Called Shrewd Judges of Risk," *New York Times*, 2 March 1993, 5(B).

9. See Ruby Takanishi, "The Opportunities of Adolescence—Research, Interventions, and Policy: Introduction to the Special Issue," *American Psychologist* 48, no. 2 (February 1993): 85–88.

10. Stuart T. Hauser and Mary Kay Bowlds, "Stress, Coping, and Adaptation," in Feldman and Elliott, *At the Threshold*, 393–96.

11. Examples include Charles M. Shelton, *Pastoral Counseling with Adolescents and Young Adults* (New York: Crossroad, 1995); G. Wade Rowatt, Jr., *Pastoral Care with Adolescents in Crisis* (Philadelphia: Westminster Press, 1989); and Richard D. Parsons, *Adolescents in Turmoil, Parents under Stress: A Pastoral Ministry Primer* (New York: Paulist Press, 1987).

12. Rodney J. Hunter, "The Future of Pastoral Theology," *Pastoral Psychology* 29, no. 1 (fall 1980): 69.

13. Charles M. Wood, *Vision and Discernment: An Orientation in Theological Study* (Atlanta: Scholars Press, 1985), 24.

Chapter 1:
The Self amid Symptoms of Youthful Despair

1. Jürgen Moltmann, *God in Creation: A New Theology of Creation and the Spirit of God*, trans. Margaret Kohl (San Francisco: Harper & Row, 1985), 28, 32ff.

2. Moltmann, *God in Creation*, 133; and Jürgen Moltmann, *The Coming of God: Christian Eschatology* (Minneapolis: Fortress Press, 1996), 23.

3. Douglas M. Meeks, *Origins of the Theology of Hope* (Philadelphia: Fortress Press, 1974), 81.

4. Jürgen Moltmann, *Theology of Hope: On the Ground and Implications of a Christian Eschatology*, trans. James W. Leitch (New York: Harper & Row, 1967), 17.

5. Cf. Moltmann, *God in Creation*, 178.

6. Moltmann, *The Coming of God*, 28.

7. Moltmann, *Theology of Hope*, 91.

8. Moltmann, *God in Creation*, 262.

9. Ben Furmann and Tapani Ahola, *Solution Talk: Healing Therapeutic Conversations* (New York: W. W. Norton & Co., 1992), quoted in Donald Capps, *Agents of Hope: A Pastoral Psychology* (Minneapolis: Fortress Press, 1995), 170.

10. Two recent volumes by noted pastoral theologians are relevant to this theme: Andrew D. Lester, *Hope in Pastoral Care and Counseling* (Louisville, Ky.: Westminster John Knox Press, 1995); as well as Capps, *Agents of Hope*.

Chapter 2:
Object Relations Theory and the Borderline Self

1. James F. Masterson, *The Search for the Real Self: Unmasking the Personality Disorders of Our Age* (New York: Free Press, 1988), 61.

2. James F. Masterson, *The Real Self: A Developmental, Self, and Object Relations Approach* (New York: Brunner/Mazel, 1985), 4; see also James F. Masterson, *The Psychiatric Dilemma of Adolescence* (New York: Brunner/Mazel, 1984 [1967]) for a lengthy summary of the original longitudinal study.

3. James F. Masterson, *Treatment of the Borderline Adolescent: A Developmental Approach* (New York: Brunner/Mazel, 1985), 19.

4. See Masterson, *The Search for the Real Self*, chs. 5 and 9.

5. Masterson, *Treatment of the Borderline Adolescent*, 23–24. Cf. also Donald B. Rinsley, *Treatment of the Severely Disturbed Adolescent* (New York: Jason Aronson, 1983), 104–10. And James F. Masterson, *Psychotherapy of the Borderline Adult* (New York: Brunner/Mazel, 1976), 43–44; and James F. Masterson, with Jacinta Lu Costello, *From Borderline Adolescent to Functioning Adult: The Test of Time* (New York: Brunner/Mazel, 1980), 10, 21–22.

6. Margaret Mahler, Fred Pine, and Anni Bergman, *The Psychological Birth of the Human Infant: Symbiosis and Individuation* (New York: Basic Books, 1975).

7. Ibid. 65, 68, 77. Cf. Masterson, *From Borderline Adolescent to Functioning Adult*, 11–14; and Masterson, *Psychotherapy of the Borderline Adult*, 34–37.

8. Masterson, *Treatment of the Borderline Adolescent*, 13, 58ff.; Masterson, *The Search for the Real Self*, 61; Masterson, *From Borderline Adolescent to Functioning Adult*, 16ff.; and Masterson, *Psychotherapy of the Borderline Adult*, 38ff.

9. Masterson, *The Search for the Real Self*, 84ff.; and Masterson, *Treatment of the Borderline Adolescent*, 43.

10. Masterson, *Treatment of the Borderline Adolescent*, 44.

11. Masterson, *From Borderline Adolescent to Functioning Adult*, 15.

12. Masterson, *The Narcissistic and Borderline Disorders: An Integrated and Developmental Approach* (New York: Brunner/Mazel, 1981), xi, 133; and Masterson, *The Real Self*, 41.

13. See, for example, Jill McLean Taylor, Carol Gilligan, and Amy M. Sullivan, *Between Voice and Silence: Women and Girls, Race and Relationship* (Cambridge: Harvard University Press, 1995), 85.

14. Jill McLean Taylor et al., *Between Voice and Silence*, 74.

15. Mary Pipher, *Reviving Ophelia: Saving the Selves of Adolescent Girls* (New York: Ballantine Books, 1994), 65.

16. Ibid., 252.

17. Ibid., 252.

18. Ibid., 37.

19. Janet Liebman Jacobs, *Victimized Daughters: Incest and the Development of the Female Self* (New York: Routledge, 1994), 21–22.

20. Masterson, *The Narcissistic and Borderline Disorders*, 131–32.

21. Ibid., 186–87.

22. Masterson, *Psychotherapy of the Borderline Adult*, 57; and Donald B. Rinsley, *Borderline and Other Self Disorders: A Developmental and Object-Relations Perspective* (New York: Jason Aronson, 1982), 60.

23. Morris N. Eagle, *Recent Developments in Psychoanalysis: A Critical Evaluation* (Cambridge: Harvard University Press, 1987), 91–92.

24. Masterson, *The Search for the Real Self*, 79.

25. Paul W. Pruyser, "What Splits in 'Splitting'?" *Bulletin of the Menninger Clinic* 39, no. 1 (January 1975): 36, 44.

26. Masterson, *The Search for the Real Self*, 77–78; and James F. Masterson, "Intensive Psychotherapy of the Adolescent with a Borderline Syndrome," in *American Handbook of Psychiatry*, 2nd ed., ed. Silvano Arieti (New York: Basic Books, 1974), 2:253–54.

27. Masterson, *Psychotherapy of the Borderline Adult*, 100–101.

28. See chapter 10, "Casework Treatment of the Parents," in Masterson, *Treatment of the Borderline Adolescent*, 141ff. The intricacies and pitfalls of this type of therapy are evident in Masterson's supervisory sessions with counseling students in James F. Masterson, *Countertransference and Psychotherapeutic Technique: Teaching Seminars on Psychotherapy of the Borderline Adult* (New York: Brunner/Mazel, 1983).

29. See chapter 5 in Masterson, *The Real Self*, 52ff., 58; also Masterson, *The Search for the Real Self*, 133–34.

30. Masterson, *The Real Self*, 26–27; and Masterson, *The Search for the Real Self*, 42–46.

Chapter 3:
The Case of Stan

1. Carl R. Rogers, *On Becoming a Person: A Therapist's View of Psychotherapy* (Boston: Houghton Mifflin Co., 1961), 26.

Chapter 4:
Self Psychology and Pathological Narcissism

1. Heinz Kohut, *Self Psychology and the Humanities: Reflections on a New Psychoanalytic Approach*, ed. Charles B. Strozier (New York: W. W. Norton & Co., 1985), 215.

2. Kohut's collected articles are found in Heinz Kohut, *The Search for the Self: Selected Writings of Heinz Kohut, 1950–1978*, 3 vols., ed. Paul H. Ornstein (Madison, Conn.: International Universities Press, 1978). His books include Heinz Kohut, *The Analysis of the Self: A Systematic Approach to the Psychoanalytic Treatment of Narcissistic Personality Disorders*, Monograph No. 4 of *The Psychoanalytic Study of the Child*, ed. Ruth S. Eissler et al. (New York: International Universities Press, 1971); Heinz Kohut, *The Restoration of the Self* (New York: International Universities Press, 1977); and Heinz Kohut, *How Does Analysis Cure?* ed. Arnold Goldberg (Chicago: University of Chicago Press, 1984).

3. See Kohut, *How Does Analysis Cure?* 87.

4. Ibid., 5, 7, 14, 16, and especially 41, 53, 87, 95, and 113. For one such critic of Kohut, see Leo Rangell, "The Self in Psychoanalytic Theory," *Journal of the American Psychoanalytic Association* 30, no. 4 (1982): 863–91. For helpful overviews of the development of Kohut's work and thought see James N. Lapsley, "The 'Self,' Its Vicissitudes and Possibilities: An Essay in Theological Anthropology," *Pastoral Psychology* 35, no. 1 (fall 1986): 23–45; and also editor Paul H. Ornstein's introduction to Kohut, *The Search for the Self*, 1:1–106.

5. Arnold M. Cooper, "Narcissism," in *Essential Papers on Narcissism*, ed. Andrew P. Morrison (New York: New York University Press, 1986), 112.

6. See Michael H. Stone's chronicle of the borderline disorder through the decades of the twentieth century, in Stone, *Essential Papers on Borderline Disorders* (New York: New York University Press, 1986), 1–13, 45–53, 149–58, 411–32.

7. Kohut, *The Search for the Self*, 2:618–19.

8. Heinz Kohut and Ernest S. Wolf, "The Disorders of the Self and Their Treatment: An Outline," in Morrison, *Essential Papers on Narcissism*, 176.

9. Kohut, *The Analysis of the Self*, 20.

10. See Cooper, "Narcissism," especially 112–15. Cf. also Christopher Lasch, *The Culture of Narcissism* (New York: Warner Books, 1979), especially 293–308; and Christopher Lasch, *Haven in a Heartless World: The Family Besieged* (New York: Basic Books, 1979), 188–89; and the now classic Kenneth

Kenniston, *The Uncommitted: Alienated Youth in American Society* (New York: Harcourt, Brace & World, 1965), 35–39, 50–51, 295–300; and David Elkind, *Ties That Stress: The New Family Imbalance* (Cambridge: Harvard University Press, 1994).

11. See Kohut, *How Does Analysis Cure?* 192–210.

12. See Kohut and Wolf, "The Disorders of the Self and Their Treatment," 177; also Kohut, *How Does Analysis Cure?* 192–93; and Kohut, *Self Psychology and the Humanities*, 217.

13. Kohut, *How Does Analysis Cure?* 52.

14. Ibid., 174.

15. Kohut, *The Search for the Self,* 1:451 footnote.

16. Kohut, *How Does Analysis Cure?* 175.

17. Kohut, *Self Psychology and the Humanities*, 222. For a critique of Kohut's claims for empathy, see Eagle, *Recent Developments in Psychoanalysis*, 64–65.

18. Kohut, *The Restoration of the Self,* 180.

19. Kohut and Wolf, "The Disorders of the Self and Their Treatment," 177.

20. Kohut, *The Analysis of the Self,* 79; Kohut, *The Restoration of the Self,* 274. For a response to Kohut's etiological position by an influential critic, see Otto F. Kernberg, *Borderline Conditions and Pathological Narcissism* (Northvale, N.J.: Jason Aronson, 1987), 162–63, 270ff.

21. Kohut, *The Analysis of the Self,* 69ff., 98–99, 121.

22. Kohut, *The Restoration of the Self,* 4, 138–39, 280ff.

23. Kohut, "Forms and Transformations of Narcissism," in *The Search for the Self,* vol. 1, especially 445ff.; and Kohut, *The Analysis of the Self,* 296ff.

24. Kohut, *How Does Analysis Cure?* 76.

25. Kohut, *The Search for the Self,* 2:617–18. See also Heinz Kohut, *The Kohut Seminars on Self Psychology and Psychotherapy with Adolescents and Young Adults,* ed. Miriam Elson (New York: W. W. Norton & Co., 1987), 3–30.

Chapter 5:
The Case of John Turner

1. Elijah Anderson, "The Story of John Turner," in *Drugs, Crime, and Social Isolation: Barriers to Urban Opportunity,* ed. Adele V. Harrell and George E. Peterson (Washington, D.C.: Urban Institute Press, 1992), 159.

2. The case also appears in Elijah Anderson, "The Story of John Turner," *Public Interest* 108 (summer 1992): 3–34. Cf. Elijah Anderson, *The Code of the Streets* (New York: W. W. Norton & Co., forthcoming). See also his chronicle of John Turner's neighborhood in Elijah Anderson, *Streetwise: Race, Class, and Change in an Urban Community* (Chicago: The University of Chicago Press, 1990). Anderson's own background afforded him special access to John Turner's domain. Born into an impoverished Mississippi Delta family of sharecroppers, Anderson moved with them in the 1940s to Indiana, where his father, with a fourth-grade education, acquired a factory job. Although Anderson himself was not of the street, he shifted easily between its language world and that of the academy. In his words, he could "talk this way, talk that way" (Ellen

K. Coughlin, "Mean Streets Are a Scholar's Lab," *Chronicle of Higher Education*, 21 September 1994, 8–9[A], 14[A], quote 9[A]). See also Elijah Anderson, "The Code of the Streets," *Atlantic Monthly*, May 1994: 81–94.

3. Anderson, in Harrell and Peterson, 149.
4. Ibid., 149.
5. Ibid., 150.
6. Ibid., 150.
7. Ibid., 153.
8. Ibid., 154.
9. Ibid., 155.
10. Ibid., 156.
11. Ibid., 157–59.
12. Ibid., 159–60.
13. Ibid., 160–61.
14. Ibid., 163.
15. Ibid., 166.
16. Ibid., 168. See also "Sex Codes and Family Life among Northton's Youth," chap. 4 of Anderson, *Streetwise*, 112–37; and Anderson, "The Code of the Streets," 89ff.
17. Anderson, in Harrell and Peterson, 168.
18. Ibid., 169.
19. Ibid., 171.
20. Ibid., 173.
21. Ibid., 173–74.
22. Anderson, "The Code of the Streets," 83.
23. Ibid., 82.
24. Anderson, in Harrell and Peterson, 177.
25. Ibid., 168.
26. Ibid., 173.
27. Ibid., 160, 166.
28. Kohut, *How Does Analysis Cure?* 18.

Chapter 6:
The Eschatological Self

1. Paul W. Pruyser, "Phenomenology and Dynamics of Hoping," *Journal for the Scientific Study of Religion* 3 (1964): 89, 92.

2. For more extensive studies comparing and contrasting various schools of depth psychology, see Fred Pine, *Drive, Ego, Object, & Self: A Synthesis for Clinical Work* (New York: Basic Books, 1990); and James F. Masterson, Marian Tolpin, and Peter E. Sifneos, *Comparing Psychoanalytic Psychotherapies: Developmental, Self, and Object Relations; Self Psychology; Short-Term Dynamic* (New York: Brunner/Mazel, 1991).

3. Frederick Buechner, "Adolescence and the Stewardship of Pain," in *The Clown in the Belfry: Writings on Faith and Fiction* (San Francisco: HarperCollins, 1992), 99.

4. See especially Joseph Weiss, Harold Sampson, and the Mount Zion Psychotherapy Research Group, *The Psychoanalytic Process: Theory, Clinical Observation and Empirical Research* (New York: Guilford Press, 1986); and Joseph Weiss, *How Psychotherapy Works: Process and Technique* (New York: Guilford Press, 1993).

5. Morris N. Eagle, *Recent Developments in Psychoanalysis: A Critical Evaluation* (Cambridge, Mass.: Harvard University Press, 1987), 97. See Joseph Weiss, "Crying at the Happy Ending," *Psychoanalytic Review* 39 (1952): 338.

6. Weiss, "Crying at the Happy Ending," 338.

7. Cf. Jay S. Efran, Michael D. Lukens, and Robert J. Lukens, *Language, Structure and Change: Frameworks of Meaning in Psychotherapy* (New York: W. W. Norton & Co., 1990), 164–65.

8. Although stemming from a quite different tradition in psychology, the concept of "conditions of safety" seems closely allied with the foundational paradox of Carl Rogers, who concluded, "[T]he more I am willing to understand and accept the realities in myself and in the other person, the more change seems to be stirred up." Change, for Rogers, arises primarily from the assurance of acceptance in the therapeutic relationship. Carl Rogers, *On Becoming a Person: A Therapist's View of Psychotherapy* (Boston: Houghton Mifflin Co., 1961), 22, 33, 76, 108.

9. Weiss, *How Psychotherapy Works*, 9.

10. Eagle, *Recent Developments in Psychoanalysis*, 98. See also Joseph Weiss, "The Emergence of New Themes: A Contribution to the Psychoanalytic Theory of Therapy," in *International Journal of Psychoanalysis* 52 (1971): 459–67.

11. Weiss, *How Psychotherapy Works*, vii.

12. For Moltmann's distinction between "interruption" as a category of historical *futurum*, and "conversion" as a category of eschatological *adventus*, see Moltmann, *The Coming of God*, 22.

13. Anderson, in Harrell and Peterson, 172.

Chapter 7:
The Case of Laurie

1. All identifying data have been altered in this case.

2. Janet Liebman Jacobs, *Victimized Daughters: Incest and the Development of the Female Self* (New York: Routledge, 1994), 144.

3. Ibid., 36–38.

4. Ibid., 35.

Chapter 8:
The Case of Bobby Griffith

1. Leroy Aarons, *Prayers for Bobby: A Mother's Coming to Terms with the Suicide of Her Gay Son* (San Francisco: HarperSanFrancisco, 1995), 125. Aarons is a noted newspaper journalist and editor (*Oakland Tribune, Washington Post*), and founder and president of the National Lesbian and Gay Journalists Association.

2. Ibid., 14.
3. Ibid., 18–19.
4. Ibid., 74.
5. Ibid., 75.
6. Ibid., 77.
7. Ibid., 45–46, 52.
8. Ibid., 52, 55.
9. Ibid., 79, 83.
10. Ibid., 88, 91.
11. Ibid., 125.
12. Ibid., 94.
13. Ibid., 101.
14. Ibid., 117, 121–22.
15. Ibid., 125, 128.
16. Ibid., 134–35.
17. Ibid., 139.
18. Ibid., 159.
19. Ibid., 161–62.
20. Ibid., 168–69.
21. Ibid., 21–23.
22. Ibid., 59, 61, 63.
23. Ibid., 66, 69, 71.
24. Ibid., 105–106.
25. Ibid., 106.
26. Ibid., 110–11.
27. Ibid., 112–115.
28. Ibid., 114–15.
29. Moltmann, *The Coming of God*, 28–29.
30. Wood, *Vision and Discernment*, 24.
31. See Carol Lakey Hess, "Abomination and Creativity: Shaking the Order of the Cosmos," *Princeton Seminary Bulletin* 15, no. 1 (1994): 28–43.
32. Questions concerning the statistical prevalence of gay and lesbian youth suicide, like most topics related to homosexuality, generate enormous controversy, in part because of the difficulty of establishing the sexual experiences or orientation of suicidal youth, who tend to withhold such information from physicians or researchers, and also given the arduous task of determining the prior sexual realities of deceased youth. In one now-famous study by the U.S. Department of Health and Human Services, authored by a gay clinical social worker and first released but then quickly withdrawn by the federal government, gay and lesbian youth were found to be two to three times more likely than heterosexual youth to attempt suicide, and to comprise up to 30 percent of all completed adolescent suicides (Paul Gibson, "Gay Male and Lesbian Youth Suicide," *Report of the Secretary's Task Force on Youth Suicide. Volume 3: Preventions and Interventions in Youth Suicide*, Department of Health and Human Services, Pub. No [ADM]89–1623 [Washington, D.C.: Supt. of Docs., U.S. Government Printing Office, 1989], 110–42). In another comparative

study, gay men were six times more likely than heterosexual men, and lesbian women twice as likely as heterosexual women, to have attempted suicide, the majority of these before the age of twenty (A. Bell & M. Weinberg, *Homosexualities: A Study of Diversity among Men and Women* [New York: Simon & Schuster, 1978]). While each side undoubtedly will continue to cite statistical evidence to support its own viewpoint, my conviction is that if even one gay or lesbian young person takes his or her life because of homosexual orientation—an act unthinkable for a youth upon discovering himself or herself to be heterosexual—then a tragic injustice has occurred.

Epilogue: Awaiting

1. Brenda Turner, "Culture Crash," *USA Weekend*, 26–28 April 1996, 5. See also Mary Pipher, *Reviving Ophelia*.

2. Wayne E. Oates, *The Presence of God in Pastoral Counseling* (Waco, Tex.: Word Books, 1986), 32, 40.

Bibliography

Aarons, Leroy. 1995. *Prayers for Bobby: A Mother's Coming to Terms with the Suicide of Her Gay Son.* San Francisco: HarperSanFrancisco.

Anderson, Elijah. 1994. "The Code of the Streets." *Atlantic Monthly,* May, 81–94.

———. 1992. The Story of John Turner. *The Public Interest* 108 (summer): 3–34.

———. 1990. *Streetwise: Race, Class, and Change in an Urban Community.* Chicago: University of Chicago Press.

Bell, A., and M. Weinberg. 1978. *Homosexualities: A Study of Diversity among Men and Women.* New York: Simon & Schuster.

Brody, Jane E. 1993. "Teen-agers' Accidents May Be Warnings of Suicide." *New York Times,* 24 March, 7(B).

Buechner, Frederick. 1992. *The Clown in the Belfry: Writings on Faith and Fiction.* San Francisco: HarperCollins.

Butterfield, Fox. 1995. "More Blacks in Their 20's Have Trouble with the Law. *New York Times,* 5 October, 8(A).

———. 1994. "Teen-Age Homicide Rate Has Soared." *New York Times,* 14 October, 10(A).

Capps, Donald. 1995. *Agents of Hope: A Pastoral Psychology.* Minneapolis: Fortress Press.

Cooper, Arnold M. 1986. "Narcissism." In *Essential Papers on Narcissism,* edited by Andrew P. Morrison, 112–43. New York: New York University Press.

Coughlin, Ellen K. 1994. "Mean Streets Are a Scholar's Lab." *Chronicle of Higher Education,* 21 September, 8–9(A) and 14(A).

Eagle, Morris N. 1987. *Recent Developments in Psychoanalysis: A Critical Evaluation.* Cambridge: Harvard University Press.

Efran, Jay S., Michael D. Lukens, and Robert J. Lukens. 1990. *Language, Structure, and Change: Frameworks of Meaning in Psychotherapy.* New York: W. W. Norton & Co.

Elkind, David. 1994. *Ties That Stress: The New Family Imbalance.* Cambridge, Mass.: Harvard University Press.

Feldman, S. Shirley, and Glen R. Elliott. 1990. *At the Threshold: The Developing Adolescent.* Cambridge: Harvard University Press.

Furmann, Ben, and Tapani Ahola. 1992. *Solution Talk: Healing Therapeutic Conversations.* New York: W. W. Norton & Co. Quoted in Donald Capps. *Agents of Hope: A Pastoral Psychotherapy.* Minneapolis: Fortress Press, 1995.

Gibson, Paul. 1989. "Gay Male and Lesbian Youth Suicide." In *Report of the Secretary's Task Force on Youth Suicide. Volume 3: Preventions and Interventions in*

Youth Suicide, Department of Health and Human Services. Washington, D.C.: Supt. of Documents, U.S. Government Printing Office (ADM 89–1623), 110–42.

Goldman, Daniel. 1993. "Teen-Agers Called Shrewd Judges of Risk." *New York Times*, 2 March, 5(B).

Harrell, Adele V., and George E. Peterson. 1992. *Drugs, Crime, and Social Isolation: Barriers to Urban Opportunity*. Washington, D.C.: Urban Institute Press.

Hauser, Stuart T., and Mary Kay Bowlds. 1990. "Stress, Coping, and Adaptation." *See* Feldman, S. Shirley, and Glen R. Elliott. 1990: 388–413.

Hess, Carol Lakey. 1994. Abomination and Creativity: Shaking the Order of the Cosmos. *Princeton Seminary Bulletin* 15, no. 1: 28–43.

Holinger, Paul C., Daniel Offer, James T. Barter, and Carl C. Bell. 1994. *Suicide and Homicide among Adolescents*. New York: Guilford Press.

Hunter, Rodney J. 1980. The Future of Pastoral Theology. *Pastoral Psychology* 29, no. 1 (fall): 58–69.

Jacobs, Janet Liebman. 1994. *Victimized Daughters: Incest and the Development of the Female Self*. New York: Routledge.

Kenniston, Kenneth. 1965. *The Uncommitted: Alienated Youth in American Society*. New York: Harcourt, Brace & World.

Kernberg, Otto F. 1987. *Borderline Conditions and Pathological Narcissism*. Northvale, N.J.: Jason Aaronson.

Kohut, Heinz. 1987. *The Kohut Seminars on Self Psychology and Psychotherapy with Adolescents and Young Adults*. Edited by Miriam Elson. New York: W. W. Norton & Co.

————, and Ernest S. Wolf. 1986. "The Disorders of the Self and Their Treatment: An Outline." In *Essential Papers on Narcissism*, edited by Andrew P. Morrison, 175–96. New York: New York University Press.

————. 1985. *Self Psychology and the Humanities: Reflections on a New Psychoanalytic Approach*. Edited by Charles B. Strozier. New York: W. W. Norton & Co.

————. 1984. *How Does Analysis Cure?* Edited by Arnold Goldberg. Chicago: University of Chicago Press.

————. 1978. *The Search for the Self: Selected Writings of Heinz Kohut, 1950–1978*. 3 vols. Edited by Paul H. Ornstein. Madison, Conn.: International Universities Press.

————. 1977. *The Restoration of the Self*. New York: International Universities Press.

————. 1971. *The Analysis of the Self: A Systematic Approach to the Psychoanalytic Treatment of Narcissistic Personality Disorders*. Monograph No. 4, *The Psychoanalytic Study of the Child*, edited by Ruth S. Eissler et al. New York: International Universities Press.

Lapsley, James N. 1986. "The 'Self,' Its Vicissitudes and Possibilities: An Essay in Theological Anthropology." *Pastoral Psychology* 35, no. 1 (fall): 23–45.

Lasch, Christopher. 1979. *The Culture of Narcissism*. New York: Warner Books.

————. 1979. *Haven in a Heartless World: The Family Besieged*. New York: Basic Books.

Lester, Andrew D. 1995. *Hope in Pastoral Care and Counseling.* Louisville, Ky.: Westminster John Knox Press.

Mahler, Margaret, Fred Pine, and Anni Bergman. 1975. *The Psychological Birth of the Human Infant: Symbiosis and Individuation.* New York: Basic Books.

Masterson, James F., Marian Tolpin, and Peter E. Sifneos. 1991. *Comparing Psychoanalytic Psychotherapies: Developmental, Self, and Object Relations; Self Psychology; Short-Term Dynamic.* New York: Brunner/Mazel.

Masterson, James F. 1988. *The Search for the Real Self: Unmasking the Personality Disorders of Our Age.* New York: Free Press.

———. 1985. *The Real Self: A Developmental, Self, and Object Relations Approach.* New York: Brunner/Mazel.

———. 1985. *Treatment of the Borderline Adolescent: A Developmental Approach.* New York: Brunner/Mazel.

———. 1984. *The Psychiatric Dilemma of Adolescence.* New York: Brunner/Mazel.

———. 1983. *Countertransference and Psychotherapeutic Technique: Teaching Seminars on Psychotherapy of the Borderline Adult.* New York: Brunner/Mazel.

———. 1981. *The Narcissistic and Borderline Disorders: An Integrated and Developmental Approach.* New York: Brunner/Mazel.

———, with Jacinta Lu Costello. 1980. *From Borderline Adolescent to Functioning Adult: The Test of Time.* New York: Brunner/Mazel.

———. 1976. *Psychotherapy of the Borderline Adult.* New York: Brunner/Mazel.

———. 1974. "Intensive Psychotherapy of the Adolescent with a Borderline Syndrome. In *American Handbook of Psychiatry,* 2d ed., vol. 2. Edited by Silvano Arieti. New York: Basic Books.

Meeks, Douglas M. 1974. *Origins of the Theology of Hope.* Philadelphia: Fortress Press.

Millstein, Susan G., and Iris F. Litt. 1990. "Adolescent Health." *See* Feldman, S. Shirley, and Glen R. Elliott, 1990: 431–56.

Moltmann, Jürgen. 1996. *The Coming of God: Christian Eschatology.* Translated by Margaret Kohl. Minneapolis: Fortress Press.

———. 1985. *God in Creation: A New Theology of Creation and the Spirit of God.* Translated by Margaret Kohl. San Francisco: Harper & Row.

———. 1967. *Theology of Hope: On the Ground and Implications of a Christian Eschatology.* Translated by James W. Leitch. New York: Harper and Row.

Morganthau, Tom, et al. 1992. "Losing Ground." *Newsweek,* 6 April, 20.

National Association of State Boards of Education. 1989. *Code Blue: Uniting for Healthier Youth.* 1012 Cameron St., Alexandria, VA 22314.

Oates, Wayne E. 1986. *The Presence of God in Pastoral Counseling.* Waco, Tex.: Word Books.

Ornstein, Paul H. 1978. "Introduction: The Evolution of Heinz Kohut's Psychoanalytic Psychology of the Self." *See* Kohut, Heinz, 1978, 1:1–106.

Parsons, Richard D. 1987. *Adolescents in Turmoil, Parents Under Stress: A Pastoral Ministry Primer.* New York: Paulist Press.

Pine, Fred. 1990. *Drive, Ego, Object, & Self: A Synthesis for Clinical Work.* New York: Basic Books.

Pipher, Mary. 1994. *Reviving Ophelia: Saving the Selves of Adolescent Girls*. New York: Ballantine Books.

Pruyser, Paul W. 1975. "What Splits in 'Splitting'?" *Bulletin of the Menninger Clinic* 39, no. 1 (January): 1–46.

———. 1964. "Phenomenology and Dynamics of Hoping." *Journal for the Scientific Study of Religion* 3:86–96.

Rangell, Leo. 1982. "The Self in Psychoanalytic Theory." *Journal of the American Psychoanalytic Association* 30, no. 4 : 863–91.

Rinsley, Donald B. 1983. *Treatment of the Severely Disturbed Adolescent*. New York: Jason Aaronson.

———. 1982. *Borderline and Other Self Disorders: A Developmental and Object-Relations Perspective*. New York: Jason Aronson.

Rogers, Carl R. 1961. *On Becoming a Person: A Therapist's View of Psychotherapy*. Boston: Houghton Mifflin Co.

Rowatt, G. Wade, Jr. 1989. *Pastoral Care with Adolescents in Crisis*. Philadelphia: Westminster Press.

Salholz, Eloise, and Gregory Cerio. 1990. "Short Lives, Bloody Deaths: Black Murder Rates Soar." *Newsweek*. 17 December, 33.

Shelton, Charles M. 1995. *Pastoral Counseling with Adolescents and Young Adults*. New York: Crossroad.

Stone, Michael H. 1986. *Essential Papers on Borderline Disorders*. New York: New York University Press.

Takanishi, Ruby. 1993. "The Opportunities of Adolescence—Research, Interventions, and Policy: Introduction to the Special Issue." *American Psychologist* 48, no. 2 (February): 85–88.

Taylor, Jill McLean, Carol Gilligan, and Amy M. Sullivan. 1995. *Between Voice and Silence: Women and Girls, Race and Relationship*. Cambridge: Harvard University Press.

Turner, Brenda. 1996. "Culture Crash." *USA Weekend*. 26–28 April, 5.

United States Department of Education. 1991. *Youth Indicators 1991*. Washington, D.C.: Government Printing Office, April.

Weiss, Joseph. 1993. *How Psychotherapy Works: Process and Technique*. New York: Guilford Press.

———, Harold Sampson, et al. 1986. *The Psychoanalytic Process: Theory, Clinical Observation and Empirical Research*. New York: Guilford Press.

———. 1971. "The Emergence of New Themes: A Contribution to the Psychoanalytic Theory of Therapy." *International Journal of Psychoanalysis* 52:459–67.

———. 1952. "Crying at the Happy Ending." *Psychoanalytic Review* 39: 338.

Wood, Charles M. 1985. *Vision and Discernment: An Orientation in Theological Study*. Atlanta: Scholars Press.

Index